Creativity
in Film

Conversations with 14 Who Excel

Creativity in Film

Conversations with 14 Who Excel

Susan Charlotte

with

Tom Ferguson and Bruce Felton

Momentum Books Ltd.

Manufactured in the United States of America

1996 1995 1994 1993   5 4 3 2 1

Momentum Books, Ltd.
6964 Crooks Road, Suite 1
Troy, Michigan 48098
USA

ISBN 1-879094-28-2

Library of Congress Cataloging-in-Publication Data

Charlotte, Susan.
    Creativity in film : conversations with 14 who excel / Susan Charlotte with Tom Ferguson and Bruce Felton.
        p.   cm.
    ISBN 1-879094-28-2 : $14.95
    1. Motion picture actors and actresses--United States--Interviews.
2. Screenwriters--United States--Interviews. 3. Motion picture
producers and directors--United States--Interviews. 4. Creation
(Literary, artistic, etc.) 5. Foote, Horton. Trip to Bountiful.
I. Ferguson, Tom, 1942- . II. Felton, Bruce. III. Title.
PN1998.2.C44 1993
791.43'092'2--dc20   93-4054
                                                          CIP

Contents

The *Trip to Bountiful* Interviews

Preface

We have the misfortune of living in an age of analysis. When we are not analyzing ourselves, we are probing the secrets of the universe. For every action there must be a reaction. For every effect there must be a cause. We have parsed ourselves into trivia. We have split the atom into quarks. We have recorded the cosmic echo of creation. But, thankfully, we have not yet explained the mystery of Creativity. Some things, apparently, are still sacred.

Nowhere is this passion for analysis more resolute than in the field of advertising. And no quest more intense than the quest for Creativity. No philosophical mystery is being sought. Just the magic ingredient that turns lead into gold.

Yet for all this analysis, nobody inside or outside advertising knows what Creativity is or how to get it. At DMB&B we knew we wouldn't be able to split this dense atom either. But we thought we might be able to define its characteristics by following the tracks it leaves in a cloud chamber.

We invited some of the most creative minds of our time to talk to us about Creativity. The stimulating conversations recorded here are far more than tracks in a cloud chamber. They are intimate glimpses into the private heaven or hell of creation by people who must endure it to make a living.

Is there a common thread? Perhaps. Or does the definition of Creativity preclude commonality? There are some fascinating clues here. While we may not find an answer we can all agree upon, a feeling slowly emerges as to what Creativity is and is not. I suspect a feeling is as close as we'll ever get to the resolution of this sublime riddle.

RON MONCHAK
Chairman, Bloomfield Hills Office
DMB&B Advertising, Inc.

Foreword

On June 25, 1987, Elmore Leonard walked into an advertising agency auditorium and talked for two hours about finding his voice as a writer. Thus was born a unique lecture series and, not indirectly, this book.

Many of the subjects who appear in the hardbound CREATIV-ITY: Conversations with 28 Who Excel were interviewed when they appeared as guest lecturers in DMB&B's ongoing Facets of Creativity Series. Some will appear in the future. Others were interviewed exclusively for the book project as we sought to mine the broadest possible vein of creative ore.

In all, we interviewed some 50 creative achievers whose disciplines range from novelist to chef to sculptor to baseball announcer. Half of them were not included in the hardbound edition, merely because of space limitations.

In the first paperback offshoot of the CREATIVITY project, we decided to zero in on a specific art form—at the same time atoning for some of our hardback sins of omission. Thus, six of our Creativity in Film subjects—including all but one of the interviews centered on The Trip to Bountiful—appear in this edition only.

The Bountiful sequence is useful not only for students and serious followers of film, but for casual moviegoers who are much less aware of the collegial nature of filmmaking.

It's important to keep in mind that creativity rather than film was the subject on the table. Most of our subjects have devoted their lives to film; consequently a reader would hardly notice the distinction. In two cases, however, actors express a preference—a strong preference—for the stage. This is hardly a surprise. And since these particular actors have been serious achievers in both stage and film, they seemed to be a logical fit.

Several potential subjects for the CREATIVITY project, from various disciplines, declined to be interviewed; but even their demurrals were often revealing and educational. Norman Mailer, for example, wrote a note to Susan Charlotte:

"I'm afraid I'm going to say no to your invitation to an interview on creativity for I think the subject is dangerous. I don't think I want to know too much about it, at least not for myself, and don't relish the idea of poking into the gears of it and possibly the wiring—it's one machine (if it is a machine) that I don't wish to get near. All I can do is wish you good luck on your book even if I'm not contributing to it."

Some of our subjects, as you will see, do not even believe themselves to be "creative." We disagree, and include them nonetheless.

These are *conversations*. We wanted to keep that flavor and texture, as much as possible in print. So there are no footnotes, and only slight parenthetical intrusion. If a few references are unknown to the reader, we apologize; on the whole this seemed to be the best way—to let the reader hear what we heard, while correcting factual slips and clarifying ambiguities wherever possible.

The first interview occurred six years ago; most were conducted in 1991 and 1992. Hence, a prolific interview subject might seem frozen in the year, or even month, of a particular conversation. On the other hand, a movie producer—working in a discipline with a similarly slow turnaround time—might find one of his projects picking up an Academy Award or two just as we go to press.

Susan Charlotte, New York playwright, screenwriter and journalist, conducted all but one of these interviews, as well as writing the precedes for her subjects. New York free-lance writer Bruce Felton interviewed Pat Collins. Felton and Tom Ferguson, managing editor of Momentum Books, copy edited the manuscript. Ferguson designed the pages.

We very much enjoyed producing this book. We hope you will enjoy reading it.

SUSAN CHARLOTTE
TOM FERGUSON
BRUCE FELTON

> **6** Change has never been hard for me. What I find difficult is no change. I think that's typical of most creative people. **9**

DAVID BROWN
Producer/Writer

David Brown is best known for producing Hollywood hits such as *Jaws, The Sting* and *Cocoon*. But he began his career as a journalist, and an eye for a story remained a long suit when he moved to the world of film and theater.

After growing up in New York and graduating from Stanford University and the Pulitzer Graduate School of Journalism at Columbia, Brown took a reporting job in San Francisco. In 1937 he returned to New York, wrote for the *New York Times* and *Women's Wear Daily* and moved on to magazines, becoming the managing editor of

David Brown: "I'm not one who can live on the coast of Maine and write a book."

Cosmopolitan in 1951. A massive career switch occurred when the head of 20th Century Fox, Darryl F. Zanuck, summoned him to Hollywood.

Brown, now a distinguished-looking man in his mid-70s, later worked with Zanuck's son, Richard, on such notable films as *The Sound of Music*, *Patton* and *The French Connection*. In 1972 they moved to Warner Brothers and set up their own company. They had an unexpected hit with *Jaws*. "We never knew whether people would laugh at the shark, because it was well-known that the shark was a mechanical one," says Brown. "That was a very big gamble."

Brown ended his partnership with Zanuck after 19 years and started his own production company, the Manhattan Project. Another of his long-term relationships seems like it will go on forever—his marriage to Helen Gurley Brown, editor of *Cosmopolitan*. They met more than 30 years ago when he was executive story editor at Fox and she was a copywriter at the Foote, Cone & Belding advertising agency.

Brown has tasted failure along with his share of success. Richard Zanuck, his future partner, fired Brown after he almost drove the studio into bankruptcy under the exorbitant costs of *Cleopatra*. And he was fired a second time by Darryl Zanuck, who thought Brown and Zanuck's own son were trying to take over the company. The son was fired, too.

Brown writes, and produces films and stageplays with no hint of stopping. At the time of this interview in his Manhattan office, Brown was preparing for a three-week trip to Europe. Part of his journey would be spent lecturing in Berlin and Madrid on the art of writing cover lines and titles—an art form he knows well after spending a quarter of a century in what he calls "his other life," journalism.

What is the most creative part of what you do?

Well, I have a multifaceted occupation. I'm a writer. I've published four books. And I'm a producer of films and plays. And occasionally I'm a journalist.

Didn't you start out as a journalist?
Indeed. You see, everything I do is creative. The perception of

producers is that they bring in the money. That's true; but basically I bring in the script, the story, the idea and then begin to assemble the numerous people required to make a movie or produce a play. So I'm involved in all aspects of the project. I guess you could say that creativity for me is a free-floating, unconscious life force.

How does your role differ in each of the various facets of your career?

As a producer in the world of entertainment, of course, you're dependent on other people—and your creativity is your ability to evaluate other people's visions, be it a script or an idea. In the theater it's the ability to respond to a completed play. But when you're writing a book you start with a blank sheet of paper. And when you read it, you cannot imagine how you got it all down; you think it was written by someone else. And then there's the creativity that comes into play when you are trying to translate a book into a film.

Which you did with *Jaws*.

And with *Cleopatra*, which to my sorrow was my suggestion.

Why to your sorrow?

Cleopatra was one of the great calamities of motion pictures. In my own memoir, called *Let Me Entertain You*, I refer to the memo at Century City—where 20th Century Fox Studios used to be. If not for *Cleopatra*, Fox would still own the land, and there's quite a chapter on that.

Aside from *Cleopatra*, are you generally good at coming up with film ideas?

Yes. I'm good at ideas and visions rather than the nitty-gritty. I'm not much on budgeting, though I am good at the bottom-line cost of a movie. And I also like to get involved with casting, although the director is the final judge of that.

What is a typical day like? Or is there no such thing in your business?

You come in the morning and no one tells you what to do. You have to start everything yourself. Once things get rolling, you have a lot of things to do. But it all starts with a blank sheet of paper.

Is it hard for you to get started?
I think starting anything that's creative is hard. It's hard to write a book. It's incredibly tedious to make a movie. Sometimes it takes years. Most of the time you're trying to convince other people of the rightness of your vision. And you may not even be able to convince yourself. It's a very difficult and stressful job. People think it's glamorous, but it isn't. And by the time it all works out you've moved on to other things. I hardly every see a movie I produce except the 90 times you look at it in the various stages of completion.

But not when it's in the theater?
No, I hardly ever look at it then. I come in after the film has been run and then I greet everyone.

How do ideas come to you?
It's hard to describe. It's more like a dream than reality. No one knows. You cannot sit down and say, "Today I'm going to think up an idea."

Do you have specific memories of an idea coming to you?
Well, the only thing I can recall of that nature—which I wrote about in my book—is when my wife and I were living in California. She was complaining about her job at an ad agency and how her ideas were not being paid attention to. I remember her describing an article she wanted to write called "The Apartment." And I thought it would be good for *Esquire*—it described her years as a single woman. And I said "Why don't you write it as a book?" That was the beginning of *Sex and the Single Girl*. That I can remember. I even recall where we had that discussion.

Where was that?
It was in the Will Rogers State Park in Palisades. And from that came not only *Sex and the Single Girl* but about five other books and *Cosmopolitan* magazine. That I can remember. As for other ideas, all I can remember is getting the idea to form my own company.

Can you talk about why you broke up with Zanuck?
Richard Zanuck and I were together, oh my, close to 30 years in one form or another. We were together with our company from 1972—about 17 years. I was 18 years older than he, and at that point in my life I wanted to do something more than I was doing within the company itself. I had no complaints about the films we made, but I wanted to make different kinds of films. And I was ready for a change.

What kind of a change?
I wanted to go into the theater and I wanted to write books. I wanted the freedom that comes with having your own company, and therefore I formed the Manhattan Project. And then a couple of years later I became president of a major company called Island World, in conjunction with making movies and TV series. And I wanted to continue writing books.

Are you the kind of person who needs change in his life?
Yes. My theory of life is that one changes things every 10 or 11 years. In this case I went almost 17 years without a basic change. When Dick and I started the Zanuck/Brown company it was liberating, because we started with nothing. And the same thing happened with the Manhattan Project. Now we have four pictures completed, including *A Few Good Men*—directed by Rob Reiner and starring Tom Cruise and Jack Nicholson—and Robert Altman's *The Player*.

What do you need to be creative? Some people need chaos, others need quiet.
I need not to be in a tranquil place. I don't think I could write in the south of France or an island in the South Pacific. I find that doesn't work for me. My most creative times are in large cities like New York or London or Tokyo.

So you need to have people around you.
Yes, that's it. I'm not one who can live on the coast of Maine and write a book. Although I can write under a tree.

What about your particular work habits? Do you use a computer or do you work with pen and paper?
I write in longhand. I don't use a word processor. I have all

the high technological stuff rusting in my apartment.

Why do you write in longhand? Do you feel closer to your work?
Exactly. I like crossing things out, and for some reason the technology gets between the creative process and myself. I've even given up the typewriter, which I used for many years. It's fatiguing. I find it easier to have a pad in my hands and start writing. Then I get someone else to type it up. Then I make a lot of changes. Then it goes to a word processor so it can be readily spewed out.

What is the difference between working with a partner and having your own company?
Dick and I were so close that we finished each other's sentences.

Like a marriage.
Exactly. I still work with partners. But I have partners for a specific project. So I have a partner in the theater, Lewis Allen, and I have several partners in the movies. I like working with a partner. It gives one an opportunity—you know, a two-against-the-world kind of thing. And you need that because as a creative person you are always living with rejection. You live mostly in an environment where most people tell you you're wrong. "The book isn't right." "The movie will never work." "Why would anyone think this play would be successful?" And most of the time the naysayers are right. But for that 20 or 30 percent of rightness you stay in the business.

How do you deal with the rejection?
You go into mourning. It's very tough. A rational person always feels like the naysayers are correct. John O'Hara told me that when one of his novels received rave reviews but a son-of-a-bitch in Indiana wrote a bad review, he always wondered if the latter was right.

So there's a period where you have to . . .
Get over the failed book, the failed movie or play. And that's tough.

Is it tougher if you have doubts within yourself about the particular project?

You always have doubts. I don't know any professional who doesn't. I was talking to Robert Altman, who's directing *The Player*, which took four years to make. It's a wonderful movie. Everyone is happy. It looks great. But Altman is a worrier and so am I. We always worry. It's very tough with a stage play; opening night at Sardi's is a killer. Maybe one out of 10 times you get a good review from Frank Rich. Then it's fun, but not usually.

Can you remember times when you had a particular vision for a film?

Yes: When we saw Peter Benchley's book *Jaws*. It seemed like it would make a good movie. But the most important part of the project was getting Steven Spielberg to direct it. Once that happened, he entered into the nuclear club of filmmakers.

What about *The Sting*?

The Sting was an almost perfect script when we saw it. But you see, in this country movies are not of an auteur nature. So as a producer you decide you want to make a movie based on a particular idea or script, like *The Sting*, and you assemble the people who will help you get it on. And then you harness your vision to the vision of the people you're working with. Whereas in the theater, the prevailing vision is that of the playwright's. You simply pray a lot! You may have an idea for casting, which you discuss. But basically it's the playwright who dominates the venture.

Do you lean more toward theater or film?

They're all my children. The theater is wonderful—it's manageable, everyone is on stage, every performance is slightly different and you have a direct relationship with the audience night after night. When you make a movie you're playing to your crew. So you haven't any idea whether the film will work.

How did you get into this work?

I guess you could say it was an accident. My real dream was to be a scientist. I was admitted to Rensselaer, and I was quite influenced by books like *Arrowsmith*, the study of the nobility of being a doctor. But all my dreams dissolved in the physics lab at

Stanford University, where I finally wound up. I couldn't get the hang of physics or higher math. It was just too tough. I was looking for something softer. And I realized that the social sciences and journalism might be an easier way to go.

So then you switched into journalism?
Yes. Journalism seemed most closely related to my need for action. I also was a news junkie and I read a lot, and as a young man I had always wanted to write. So I started writing for the school paper, *The Stanford Daily*. Everything I've done since that time relates to the written word, even though it's now on film or in the theater and it's spoken and visualized. I got into this work through my preoccupation and interest in writing.

Are there any writers in your family?
No. My father was one of the early public relations men. The only book he wrote he paid to have published.

Can you talk about when you were editing *Cosmopolitan* and Darryl F. Zanuck invited you to Fox?
I was going through a painful divorce—is there any other kind? And I received a telephone call from my agent in New York, Carl Brandt. He said, "Zanuck is looking for the best editor in New York and I've suggested you." I later learned that I was one of three—the editor of the *Saturday Evening Post* was also being considered. Zanuck wanted an editor to come to Hollywood to be his chief creative aide and to run the studio in much the same manner as a national magazine. At the time there were 28 producers under contract, plus directors and stars.

When was that?
1951. Without telling anyone at work, I snuck out to Hollywood pleading a family emergency in San Francisco. I visited Darryl Zanuck, whom I had met as a journalist, and had lunch in his dining room with all his producers. I never went into his office. After lunch he simply said, "Tell Joe Moskowitz (who was Zanuck's vice-president in New York) to make a deal with you." And that's how I came to Hollywood.

So you didn't have a background in films.
Not at all. I had to take a crash course, in a sense. Times were

different. People didn't kill to get into movies. They went to Hollywood to make money so they could get back and write the great American novel or play.

How did the people in New York respond?

Dick Berlin, who was my boss, said he'd offer me as much money to stay. But as I said, I was going through a divorce and I thought it would be a good change of life. So off we went to L.A. and that was the beginning of my movie career.

How did you respond when you first got to Hollywood?

It was wonderful. It was the Golden Age. Nunnally Johnson said, "They're very forgiving out here. They don't expect anything for two or three years, so don't be discouraged if only part of your ideas are accepted."

Can you talk about your relationship with Zanuck?

He was my mentor. And it was wonderful to be around him because he was immensely creative, a person of wild enthusiasms. He took on the aura of the second coming. I like the fact that he was always on the positive side. When he criticized a script, usually he would start by telling what was good about it, and then he would go into details about what he would do to improve it. I also liked the fact that he was action-oriented—let's do it now.

When he commented on a script would you meet with him in his office or would he call you on the phone?

He commented entirely by memorandum, almost never by telephone. He had an office boy who stood by properly attired, in a jacket and tie, if you can imagine that in Hollywood. The boy would get on his bicycle and deliver Zanuck's notes immediately. He never kept files. He had his secretary type comments like, "Fine, go ahead." Or, "Make the best deal you can but don't lose it." Then he would go into a long memorandum in which he would analyze our mistakes—but he would say they were his mistakes, not yours. I liked that about him. I also liked the fact that he was genuinely a cosmopolitan person. He didn't just live in Hollywood. His world was much broader. He spent three months a year in Europe and had friends everywhere.

Can you talk about working with his son?

Dick and I were partners, but Darryl was my boss. Dick has a lot of the traits of his father but he's much more practical. He's more of a realist. He worried about his father's enthusiasms and rightly so.

Why is that?

Because some of Darryl's choices were not good and we had some terrible bombs. So Dick became much more practical.

Do you feel you need both—enthusiasm and a sense of realism?

Yes. But times were different when Darryl was producing. I don't think he could have survived in today's world.

In what sense?

The film business is now a world of super agents and actors who dictate how a script should be written. In Darryl's world the story was the primary element in the film. If he were working today he would have to make a profound change. On the other hand, Dick grew up in a Hollywood that was in rapid transition, where the actors were not under contract. It was no longer possible to cast a movie by a chart on your desk which showed that you could put Betty Grable here and Don Ameche there.

And you lived through both.

Yes. I lived in the old Hollywood and I'm right now red-hot deeply involved in the new Hollywood. Dick is old enough to remember the old Hollywood but he wasn't working in that world. When I started working for his father, Dick was still a student at Stanford University.

Has it been hard for you to make the transition from the old to the new Hollywood?

Change has never been hard for me. What I find difficult is no change. I think that's typical of most creative people. I couldn't function where everything is stagnant.

What's the greatest challenge for you?

Staying alive! Number two is finding a wonderful script. Most of them are garbage.

How have you changed?

One gets more secure in one's responses; one becomes less secure in one's knowledge. You know that almost every problem has been faced before. And you realize that all you're making is a movie. It's not life and death, which is what it feels like in all young careers. There's such anxiety about making it in today's world. In the words of Alan J. Lerner, "I'm glad I'm no longer young." It's a tough world, and I feel for these kids who are trying to break in. Especially when I think of how accidentally I got in, with very little background in the film business itself.

Theater is also much different now. How has that affected you?

It costs so much to get a play going. You hardly ever think of Broadway.

Though you have had several Broadway hits.

Yes, I produced *Tru* with Lewis Allen and *A Few Good Men*, which Rob Reiner and I have made into a movie. And I did a play called *The Cemetery Club*, which wasn't a success in the theater but which I'm now turning into a movie. The point is, it costs so much to get a play on stage that you just can't produce that many.

You once said in an article, "I'm an incomplete person working against time." Do you still feel that way?

I don't remember saying that, but I'll take credit for it. Actually, I'd say everyone is incomplete. But I'm more complete now than I've ever been.

Do you still feel you're working against time?

No. I don't feel what I'm doing has to be finished or the world will be a less perfect place. My friend John O'Hara did feel that way, because he had a medical condition. If I were Mozart or a major novelist with a big work in progress, then I'd be working under a time constraint—but everything I do is fairly short-term.

Whose opinion matters most to you?

My wife's, but not on movie matters.

Should I ask on what matters?
On plain matters of surviving and just on life and how you feel about things and people. I'd say she's an important influence.

What about movie matters?
I'll appropriate the words of Darryl Zanuck, immodest as they are: "I listen to myself. Always." I'm subject to other people's opinions because I have to go out and get approvals in order to get money. But I listen to myself. When I haven't listened to myself, I've been wrong. And sometimes when I have listened I've also been wrong. But I prefer it that way because I wouldn't know how else to play it. It's the only reliable barometer I have.

What do you feel your limitations are?
I suppose not being thorough enough in my analysis of a script on a first reading. Sometimes I'm impulsive, and after reading something for the second time I say, "My God, is that what I liked?" Or after seeing a film I might think, "Is this what we've been working on?"

When you think back on your most successful projects, what do you think was most helpful to you? Would you say it was your experience?
Actually it was the opposite; it was my naivete.

How so?
I remember being interviewed by David Susskind right after Dick and I produced *Jaws*. We both agreed that a certain naivete and innocence is necessary to successfully participate in this business. Because if you knew what you were up against, you wouldn't venture into so many dangerous places. You could say I share Ruth Gordon's philosophy, "Never, ever face the facts."

When did you venture into dangerous places?
When Dick and I produced *Jaws*. Had we read the story carefully we never would have acquired the book rights, because we would have thought it was an impossible film to make. How do you make a movie in which a shark jumps onto the stern of a

boat and swallows a man? How do you do that? There's a certain need not to be practical and not to be so bloody certain. You have to be able to take a risk based on emotion or creativity or whatever you want to call it. And so I think a liability can become an asset.

But you're not naive now.
Yes I am. I'm still naive. I mean, some harebrained scheme is just as likely to get me going now. Perhaps what is most important to being a creative producer is protecting your innocence. When I read a script it's as though I were a moviegoer, not a producer.

So, in a way, you have to put all that you know and all your experience aside.
Yes. I believe that experience does not necessarily count except in very pragmatic and specific things. I know, for example, when someone writes in a script, "The Indians burned the fort down," that two weeks of shooting might be in that one sentence. But experience would not lead one to some of the greatest hits of our time, because you might say this would never work. But times change and it does work.

Do you have any regrets?
I don't think in those terms. I think you'll find most creative people don't think about their failures. They think the public is wrong.

And is that what you think?
Probably not as much as most people. Actually, I usually think the public is right, that the public knows. I guess you could say my one regret is that I didn't make more out of my career in journalism. I like that very much. I came into entertainment accidentally. I enjoyed it, but I still kept my hand in the world of news.

If you were to come back in another lifetime would you return to journalism?
Yes. My ambition in another life would be to become the editor of *The New Yorker*, *Esquire* or *Time*. Frequently in life it's a choice between wants; and one can't have everything.

> ❝ It's treacherous business for a critic to go in and bring anything personal to the table or to be anything other than ruthlessly objective and honest when you evaluate a movie. Even a nice guy is capable of making a bomb—and when he does, you have to tell it like it is. ❞

PAT COLLINS
Film Critic

Something is mildly awry with the idea of interviewing Pat Collins at 9 o'clock on a sunny morning. As arts and entertainment editor of superstation WWOR-TV, Collins reviews movies and interviews Hollywood celebrities several times a week. Millions of viewers in 48 states see her work, but never before 10 or 11 p.m. Like Leno and Koppel, she's a fixture of TV's nocturnal landscape and isn't pictured as having a daytime life.

Reviewing movies, however, is only part of what Pat Collins does.

Pat Collins: "I have no desire to write, direct or act in movies any more than most sportswriters want to be athletes."

A big part, to be sure—but not the whole nine yards. Five days a week she commutes to Manhattan from her home in Westchester County to help run two businesses—Jonico Music, which handles the interests of her late husband, composer-lyricist Joe Raposo, who died in 1989; and Music Publishing International, which produces and markets recordings of many artists. Both companies are housed in the ninth-floor studio in Carnegie Hall where our interview took place.

Raised in suburban Boston, Collins was hired out of college as a reporter for the Boston *Record American*. "I got to do a little of everything," she recalled. "I covered crime, politics, even theater." During a newspaper strike, she was recruited to read her reviews on TV; that led to her first TV assignment, as co-host of *Panorama*, a live three-hour talk-and-information program in Washington, D.C. She hasn't worked in print journalism since. "I don't miss it at all," she said.

Over the next few years, Collins hosted issues-oriented talk shows, reviewed movies, and anchored the news at TV stations in Washington, San Francisco and Boston. After a two-year stint as a network correspondent for NBC in the early 1970s, she moved to WCBS-TV in New York, where she produced and hosted *The Pat Collins Show*.

This was daytime TV with a brain. In-depth reporting on topics like homosexuality in professional sports and deafness in children were typical fare. *The Pat Collins Show* received two Emmys, including one for the best public affairs and information program of 1976. Collins added a third Emmy a few years later as arts and entertainment reporter for CBS Morning News. She joined WWOR in 1987.

At 48, Collins could be the model for what one women's magazine calls "a juggler"—a woman who has built a successful career and raised a family without shortchanging either. Several years ago, she and Raposo and their four children gave up their Fifth Avenue apartment and moved to Westchester.

"The city is a great place to live and work, but it can also be a scary place to raise children," she said. "I suppose if we only had one child, it would have been easier, but with four, the chances of their running into trouble are that much greater."

It isn't surprising that helping her children find a safe—but not sterile—path through the jungle of TV and movie fare has been an especially compelling priority.

"I've never felt I could be totally laissez-faire with my kids about what they could see," she said. "But I also couldn't very well tell my kids that TV was garbage and then spend three-quarters of my waking hours looking at it or appearing on it."

"We've got seven TV sets in the house, and I decided long ago to make the media work for us. Every Saturday night since Elizabeth and Andrew [now in their teens] were old enough to crawl we've had Saturday night movies. It's a tradition we started in the days before videocassettes, but we had a projector. One week we'd have a Charles Laughton festival, another week it would be Hitchcock—or the Marx Brothers."

Do you ever have second thoughts when your reaction to a film runs counter to everyone else's? Do you stop and ask yourself, "What am I missing?"

No. Film reviewing isn't a poll. As a reviewer you have your own set of standards and apply them to each film, and if the movie doesn't meet those standards, you say so, regardless of what everyone else might be saying. Period. It doesn't matter to me one bit that I might be a minority of one on a given film—that I may like something everyone else hates, or vice versa.

I recall that happening with *Regarding Henry*. When it came out in 1991, no one seemed to have a kind word to say about it—except you. How come?

I did like *Regarding Henry*, and I have a theory about why no one else did. I think the critics were angry at Mike Nichols for being too *sentimental*. Mike has always given us movies with an edge, whether it's *Carnal Knowledge* or *The Graduate* or *Catch-22*. But with *Working Girl*, which was basically a Staten Island Cinderella story, he began to put more sentiment in his movies, a characteristic one doesn't normally associate with Mike Nichols.

Regarding Henry took the sentimentality a step further, and I think the critics felt let down—same as if you went to an Arnold Schwarzenegger film and he acted out of character, or didn't say any of those one-liners you expect from him. They said, wait a minute—I expect something when I watch a Mike Nichols film and I'm not getting it. I hate it.

So reviewers typically bring to their job a certain set of expectations?

We all do. When you go to a film by Stephen Spielberg or Alfred Hitchcock, or with Robin Williams, don't you have very specific expectations? How could you not? The same holds true if you see a movie based on a novel. You form mental images of scenes and characters and expect they will be depicted on the screen just as you imagine them. That's why I make a point not to read best-sellers or any other books that are likely to be made into movies. I want to come to a movie with as few preconceptions and expectations as possible.

But if Mike Nichols wants to make sentimental movies—or if Arnold Schwarzenegger wants to do *Twelfth Night*—he has an absolute right to do so. And the critics have an absolute obligation to judge him solely on the merits of the performance and not by the expectations they bring to the screening room. If the effort turns out to be a disaster, of course, you say so. At the same time, it would be unfair to blast a Spielberg or a Mike Nichols when you might go easier on a novice director making his debut and turning out the same movie.

Do you ever revisit a film and revise your original opinion?

If you're asking do I ever go back to a movie and change my mind about it, no. I can think of no time when I blasted a film and then went back later and said, "Oh, I see what he was trying to do. Not bad."

However, I think most people, myself included, sometimes go back to old movies that we saw and loved in childhood, and realize they're not that wonderful. It's a little like going back to your hometown: You visit your high school auditorium, which seemed like the biggest place in the world when you were a kid—only now that you've seen Lincoln Center or the Royal Albert Hall, it looks the size of your bathroom.

But doesn't that principle also work in reverse? When we go back to movies as adults, don't we sometimes see things we missed when we were younger?

Of course. Think about all the Bergman films we saw in college. Being Psych 101 students and totally ego-centered, we'd see the movie entirely in terms of our own lives. And we'd pay very close attention to all the *symbolism* of it. But I find that when I go back to Bergman as an adult, I pay much less attention to all those heavy symbols, and more attention to the visual aspects of his films—the way scenes are shot and how the shots work.

Are movies today as good as they were a generation or two ago?
I think the really good movies now—*Dances with Wolves*, say, or *Terms of Endearment*—are as good as the really good movies of the past. Maybe better. When it comes to full-blown, sweeping epics, for example, I think *Dances with Wolves* stands up against anything done by David Lean. I think he would have been proud to have his name on a movie with such majesty and sweep.

As for the general run of movies and whether they compare with what Hollywood was turning out in the 1930s and '40s— well, that's another story. I think a big change in the movie business took place when the studio system was dismantled. Back when you had great artists like Frank Capra, or Tracy and Hepburn under contract to one studio or another, you could get three and four movies out of them a year. Naturally, the more opportunities they had to come to bat, the more likely they'd be to turn in memorable performances and make memorable movies.

There is also too much emphasis on special effects today, often at the expense of good writing. The simple truth is that special effects can't make a movie; if the writing isn't good, the movie won't be. When a Spielberg directs, he knows exactly who's going to say what at what point, and that's critically important. It all has to be down there on paper; you can't make up a movie as you go along. When a director allows his cast to improvise, you're in for a bumpy ride.

When you speak of "great artists," how do you define the term?
Range and versatility are absolutely essential. There is also believability, or what Spencer Tracy was talking about when he said, "Don't let them catch you acting."

For instance, I don't fall in line with everyone who thought Dustin Hoffman was brilliant in *Rain Man*. I thought his performance wasn't so much acting as it was an acting exercise; you could imagine him saying to himself, "I'm going to take this difficult and unusual character and make it even more difficult and unusual on the screen."

You don't consider that great acting?

No. I think it's much more difficult to do what, say, Gene Hackman does in movies like *The Conversation* or *The French Connection*, or *Mississippi Burning*, which is to take an ordinary guy—a cop, an FBI agent—and make him memorable. Gene Hackman is my personal favorite among actors living today. You can see him in your mind, even as I'm talking about him; he does such little things with such deftness, and just throws them away. You forget it's Gene Hackman; *you can't catch him acting.* DeNiro too—when he's working, he *is* the taxi driver, he *is* Jake LaMotta. I wouldn't say that about a lot of other people up there on the screen today. They may be stars but they're not great actors.

Who, for example?

Julia Roberts, for one. I'm not sure she's a great actress, and the jury is still out as to whether she'll ever be one. That she is a movie star, however, is not in question. And since movies are so indisputably a *visual* medium—it all has to happen up there on the screen—you have to have people audiences want to look at. There has to be something about them that makes you want to watch.

Tom Cruise is another good example. Even though he has yet to make the movie that says he's a great actor, I find I want to watch him. And it goes beyond physical attractiveness. There is something about his smile and his personal appeal that's visually arresting. And that's what movies are about.

Do your personal relationships with actors or directors ever influence the way you review a movie?

Never. It's treacherous business for a critic to go in and bring anything personal to the table or to be anything other than ruthlessly objective and honest when you evaluate a movie. Even a nice guy is capable of making a bomb—and when he does, you have to tell it like it is.

Isn't it difficult to remain above the fray when you have friends in the movie industry?

Actually, I don't have many friends in the business for that very reason. One of the exceptions, though, is Gene Wilder. [My husband] Joe and I were friends with Gene and Gilda [Radner];

today, he and I share the common experience of losing our spouses to cancer within the space of a year. So I have deep feelings for Gene, as well as a lot of respect for him and for his work. But that didn't stop me from giving a deservedly unfavorable review to his latest movie.

Which one was that?
Another You. It was his third movie with Richard Pryor, and it was just painful to sit through. Not only didn't it work as a film, it had the extra problem of Richard's poor health; he had bypass surgery right after they finished shooting, and his illness was obvious throughout the movie. You don't have to be Michael DeBakey to look at this movie and say, here is a man in a lot of pain who needs to be in a hospital, and not in a movie. So a situation like this puts you in a tough situation as a critic, but you can't let those factors influence your judgment.

I'll give you another example—Mel Brooks. He's also turned out a major bomb this year, called *Life Stinks.* I call it a bomb because, guess what—homelessness is not funny, not on any level. Maybe 20 years from now, when we've either solved, or at least begun to cope more effectively with homelessness, we can treat it with some humor in the way *M.A.S.H.* looks back at Korea and sees something funny in what was a great tragedy. I admire Mel Brooks and like him personally, but you cannot bring those feelings to the table. It's fatal if you do.

I imagine there are critics who aren't so objective.
Of course. They go in with an agenda. Some critics will give a good review in the hope of being invited to the director's beach house or his next party or to return a favor. It happens all the time. And they are making a terrible mistake. Being a critic sometimes puts you in the position of having to say bad things about good people, and there is often the temptation to say to yourself, "Gee, his performance wasn't very good, but he's a nice guy so I'll ease off on him." But it's a temptation you have to resist.

I imagine you make people angry from time to time.
Perhaps. But you can't let that influence you. Joe didn't have a critic's mentality—since he was working the same side of the street as a composer or director or even an actor, he tended to be

more generous. I don't enjoy that luxury. Once, at a party, just after we were married, Hal Prince came up to us and said, "Joe—you've gone over to the enemy." It was a joke, but not without its bite.

At the same time, I don't think you have to bring out the sledge hammer with every review you do, although I do have a few colleagues who favor that style. These are people who have built their reputation on relentlessly savage criticism. Frankly, I think it makes them sound very one-note.

Presumably the temptation to really sock it to a performer you don't like is also pretty strong.

It can be, particularly when you're dealing with someone who isn't very nice. I'm not big on Madonna, and I view her as little more than a very adept piece of marketing. But *Truth or Dare* is an expertly done documentary, and I said so in my review. Now, maybe that's more to the director's credit than hers. But the lesson, obviously, is that you cannot go to a Madonna movie with the thought, "Well, I hate Madonna so I've made up my mind that I'm not going to like it." You shouldn't be a critic if that's how you view a film.

How many movies do you see a year?

Maybe 275. But I try to bank them, so that I get in three movies a day. That way, I can keep the screenings from interfering too much with the other parts of my professional life—especially since I'm here in the office every day on Jonico business.

Do you take notes as you watch?

Yes. Not copious notes, but enough to write a review. After the screening, I rush back to the office and make sure the notes are clear and complete, because it may be a month before I actually do the review on camera.

You've written and produced TV specials of your own. Do you ever feel the urge to make movies yourself?

No, thanks. I have no desire to write, direct or act in movies any more than most sportswriters want to be athletes. I'm very happy as a critic.

Do you always see movies at screenings, or do you ever buy

a ticket and see a movie like the rest of us?

Almost always at screenings. I know it sounds elitist, but there are two very practical reasons. First, if you like a movie, the movie companies will want quotes from you for their advertising campaign, which means you need to see the film before it opens in the theaters.

Second, it's hard to watch a film critically in a movie theater. People tend to talk back at the screen. They bring basket lunches and drown out the dialogue with the sound of their chewing. Or they laugh at inappropriate times—when someone is dying, or during an especially poignant scene that makes them uncomfortable. But the talking is the worst. It makes it very hard to watch a film critically. I suppose we've gotten so used to talking back to our TV sets that we forget that it's not OK to talk back to the movie screen.

Then obviously you're not a total stranger to movie theaters.

Well, I do see movies in theaters from time to time—with my kids, certainly. I chose to see *Boyz N the Hood* like a civilian, because I wanted to see how the crowd responded to the movie. Movie companies all think that crowds influence the critic, that if the public loves the movie, the critics will follow. It's one of the major fictions, but this was one time when I thought that public reaction to a movie was worth noting.

As it turned out, it was the theater's reaction to the audience that struck me. I saw it at one of the East Side Manhattan theaters near Bloomingdale's. It's an especially badly run theater—one that isn't used to getting a lot of blacks. Mostly, the audiences are white, trendy, and upscale. The staff there was so rude to the predominantly black audience I wanted to strangle the manager. They were awful.

I imagine that one of the occupational hazards of your line of work is having to sit through a lot of terrible movies. Do you ever walk out in the middle?

Never. It's a matter of principle. No matter how bad a movie is, you just never know. Maybe in the last 10 seconds, somebody will appear on screen who is absolutely wonderful. They won't save the movie, but you ought to see the performance.

What about seeing a really good movie a second time?

Again, the answer is never. Or almost never. I'm not talking about classics like *Citizen Kane* or *A Night at the Opera*, which I can watch over and over. But as for recent movies, there's just too much stuff and too little time.

I saw *Home Alone* a second time because my kids and I found ourselves in a hotel room with one of those pay-per-view TVs. And I saw *Dances with Wolves* a second time because I wanted them to see it and I knew they wouldn't go on their own.

What kind of movies do you dislike the most?
The "slice-and-dicers"—the Freddy Krueger movies, the *Friday the 13th* series, and so forth. Actually, I made it a point to see quite a number of slice-and-dicers a few years back when I was campaigning to get the rating system changed—and, in particular, to get the "R" category overhauled. Not that I was successful. You can't get Jack Valenti to budge on very much, and certainly not on the rating system.

What's the problem with the "R" rating?
It's much too inclusive. How can a charming movie like *Stand by Me*, or even a comedy like *Beverly Hills Cop*, be put in the same category with *Friday the 13th*? This isn't helpful to the moviegoer, or to parents trying to decide which films are appropriate for their kids. People thought the problem was fixed when Hollywood came out with the "NC-17" category a few years ago. But "X" and "NC-17" are insignificant ratings from the consumer point of view, because so few people go to either type of movie. Yes, I understand the serious directors who lobbied for the creation of the "NC-17" rating because they didn't want to be lumped with the dirty movies on Eighth Avenue. But the category that's really in trouble is "R."

What's so terrible about the "slice-and-dicers?"
I think all the violence and the way it's presented has a particularly dehumanizing effect on viewers—especially pre-adolescents. And these movies present sex not only as dirty and wrong—but as an act of revenge. For pre-adolescents, interestingly, seeing all the Freddy Krueger movies has become more of a rite of passage—a required demonstration of pubescent machismo.

When I was at CBS News I did a series of reports based on a

University of Wisconsin research study on the effect of slice-and-dice movies on young males in the 14-20 range. The major effect was an appalling disregard for women—which is hardly surprising. Women in these movies are almost always the victims and almost always disrobed or half-robed when they are attacked, leading to the inference that somebody dressed that way deserves what she gets.

How was the data collected?

The researchers set up mock rape trials. Beforehand, one group of jurors would be shown a couple of these "slice-and-dicers"; a control group would view a Hepburn-Tracy movie or something similar. None of the test subjects was aware that the specific movies they saw were intended to influence their reaction as jurors or even that their viewing the film had any connection with the trial.

Remarkably, every time, without exception, the "slice-and-dice" jurors would rule in favor of the defendant on the grounds that he was within his rights because the victim was "asking for it." Conversely, the control group always voted to convict. The study demonstrated in convincing and chilling terms what a profound effect movies have on how we view our fellow human beings, and specifically on the effect they have on young impressionable people.

What does a critic have to be conscious of while viewing a film?

Like an actor or director, a critic has to pay attention to his or her audience. Who are they? Where do they live? Which movies are they watching? For all the stir it created in Cannes and New York when it opened, a film like *Barton Fink*, say, isn't a factor in most of the world. WWOR is a superstation, which means I'm seen in 48 states, and the fact that we're on a satellite feed puts us in 105 smaller markets around the country, and in most of those places they don't know nor do they care about *Barton Fink*. And why would they? It created a big stir at Cannes, and made John Turturro a hot item for 10 minutes, but as far as most of the moviegoing public is concerned, it doesn't even register on the Richter scale.

The New York media like to discover people. It's the kingmaker theory: I'm important if I discover somebody. So they pro-

mote an actor, and if he then goes on to make it, it's a self-fulfill-
ing prophecy, not to mention very flattering to their ego. I'm not
into that kind of thing.

**Do you ever find yourself not knowing what to say about a
movie?**

Never. Oh, there are times when I'll have a mixed opinion:
The lead actor was wonderful, but the movie didn't pull it
together . . . or the director knew what he wanted to do, but in
the backup department—scriptwriting, special effects, whatever—
he didn't get the support he needed.

But I would never *not* have an opinion. When you're a critic,
that's not allowed.

❝ If you can see a character when you're reading a script, if you can visualize that character in your mind and then make yourself fit that visualization, that's primarily all you need. **❞**

MORGAN FREEMAN

Actor

From the *Taming of the Shrew* at the Public Theatre, to *The Three Musketeers* with Kevin Costner in London, to a possible trip to Africa, then back to New York instead on his way to an island in the West Indies, and finally to the Academy Awards in Hollywood: This was the schedule into which Morgan Freeman was asked to fit an interview.

When that conversation finally took place nine months later, he downplayed his own part in the creative process.

Freeman started his acting career in the third grade when he was the lead in *Little Boy Blue*. Four years later he won his first acting award. "I was such a scene stealer," he once said. "The other students all wanted to give me manicures and comb my eyebrows."

Morgan Freeman, drawn from *The Mighty Gents*.

His mother made him feel he could do anything. "When I see what I want, I don't see the barriers." And what he wanted was to be the first black man to win an Oscar. Though Sidney Poitier was that man, Freeman has fared quite well—three Obies, a Drama Desk award, one Tony and two Oscar nominations.

Success did not come overnight in a career that took him back and forth between California and New York. He worked with a small musical company, but when he refused to play the role of an American Indian—a role he thought was patronizing—he was fired. He took a job in the post office, then returned to New York and a job as a dancer at the 1964 World's Fair. His first real break was in 1967, in a play called *The Niggerlovers* with Stacey Keach and Viveca Lindfors. His first commercial success was *Hello Dolly* with Pearl Bailey. He then landed the title role of *Easy Rider* on a Public Television children's show. The money got better, but he didn't feel challenged. Freeman started drinking, then stopped when he fainted on the show.

In 1976 he returned to the stage and received Obies for Shakespeare's *Coriolanus* and *The Gospel at Colonus*. In 1978 he won his first Tony nomination, for *The Mighty Gents*, written by Richard Wesley. He was 40 years old and soon he hit a rough patch. After almost 10 years of not working, he landed several roles, including *Driving Miss Daisy*, *Glory*, *Lean on Me*, *Taming of the Shrew* and *Streetsmart*, which earned him his first Oscar nomination.

You once said that "changing roles is like stepping over a crack. It's not how wide it is, it's how deep it is." How did you go from an easygoing, caring chauffeur in *Driving Miss Daisy* to a volatile, sadistic pimp in *Streetsmart* without falling into the crack?

I don't know how to talk about how I make those transitions or how I do what I do. I just do it.

What attracts you to the process?
There's a joy for me. It's in doing my best to embody a character.

Edward Zwick, who directed you in *Glory*, said you don't

just perform a role, you inhabit it. Do you have any sense of how you do that?

I try to get as far away from the physical me as possible.

Away from yourself?

Just your physical self. You never really get away from the real you. The parts you play are just different aspects of the total person, of yourself.

Including the character in *Streetsmart*? Was he also a part of you?

Of course that was me. That was an aspect of my own personality that I was able to just unleash because it was safe.

Because you were acting.

Right.

So the part was not hard for you to play?

No, it was one of the easiest jobs I've ever had.

Weren't you once in a gang called the Spiders?

Way back—when I was a kid.

And you said you hated being in a gang because you found it too painful to cause pain.

That's right.

But in *Streetsmart* that's all you were doing.

I caused no pain in that movie. It all was pretend. Everything about it was pretend. One of the things that pleases me quite a lot is that actors and actresses have said they like working with me because I'm safe. I don't need to hurt you to make it look good. I believe totally in acting. It's about acting, it's not about being real.

What are some of your favorite roles?

The two that you mentioned—*Driving Miss Daisy* and *Streetsmart*.

What appealed to you about each of them?

Well, with *Miss Daisy*, I had a connection to it. I loved the character of Hoke. I knew him and I knew Miss Daisy. I knew them because they're Southerners and I'm from the South myself.

From Mississippi.
Right. I was born in '37 and I grew up in the '40s and '50s. So the era of the movie was my era. I knew what the dance was down there, how these people acted, how the social intercourse was handled. Alfred had gotten every beat of it; it was all there.

You're talking about Alfred Uhry, the playwright?
Right. The story was very recognizable and it was clear that he was writing about somebody he cared about.

You wanted to do that part before you even read the script, didn't you?
Yes, I wanted to do it as soon as I read a synopsis at Playwrights Horizons. And they picked me.

What was the difference between working with Dana Ivey on stage and Jessica Tandy in the film?
The major difference is that Dana is from Atlanta. And like me she had a much more intimate relationship with that character in her being, in her self. She fully understood the dance, so she knew where that woman came from and where she went to in that relationship.

And that had a great impact on your work?
Absolutely.

Did you enjoy working with Jessica Tandy?
Oh heavens, yes: I just fell in love with her. She's just such a professional and gracious lady, let me tell you. And a wonderful actress.

What do you do when you're first getting ready for a role?
I just read the script. And then I use my intuition. I guess you could say that there are two things I find generally will cement a character, and that is costume and makeup. If you can see a character when you're reading a script, if you can visualize that char-

acter in your mind and then make yourself fit that visualization, that's primarily all you need.

When you talk about fitting that visualization, is that part of getting as far away from the physical you as possible?
Exactly.

And you were able to do that with both those parts—to see the characters?
Yeah. When we did *Streetsmart* the whole character hinged for me on the costume, and when I told the costume designer about that she was in full agreement. She practically spent her whole budget on what I wanted.

So you had a lot of say in designing his whole look—his gold tooth, his nails and all the rest?
Yeah, I had everything to say. They gave me that character. Jerry Schatzberg was the director, and he told everyone to give me whatever I wanted.

What about the way you walk? You had one particular walk with *Streetsmart* and a whole different walk with *Driving Miss Daisy*. Do you work on that, or does that come naturally?
No, you work on everything. It comes as a package. You put on the costume and you stand looking at yourself and you start fitting yourself into it. You know a pimp is gonna walk a certain way. A street dude, a street person—these guys have a certain hippity-dippity walk.

You did not make that role into a caricature. And that could easily have happened.
- I try desperately not to do caricatures.

How do you get away from that—especially when you're doing a character like a pimp? You have a certain image of what a pimp might be like, and yet he was his own character.
You have to come back to the director. I need him to give me carte blanche so I can find the character that the writer has created.

And that's how you stay away from doing caricatures?

Yes, I try to live up to the writer's vision. Because he's the one who's really creating.

You don't feel you're creating?

No, actors are not really creating. The writer has done the creative work. There is a character already there, there is a story already there. Maybe he hasn't fleshed out the character, but if he's done the story the character is there. Or maybe he's got extra character and the story needs a little more work. But still it's the writer who has done the basic work. You're building on that—if you're doing anything at all.

What about the other actors—what do you need from them?

I think actors need actors. Let's go to *Streetsmart*. There's a scene in there with Cathy Baker when I have a scissors right under her eye. People have told me it was the most frightening scene. But you know what you were looking at? You were looking at fear, the fear on Cathy's face.

Someone wrote that originally it wasn't shot that way, with the camera on her face. That you were the one who made the suggestion.

No. The director did shoot it that way so you could see her face; but you could also see my face. So I merely said to him, "You're not gonna need this shot when you come around and look at my face because all of it is right there on her face." He agreed when he looked at it. I mean you think I hurt her, but it's really all her doing. 'Cause I didn't hurt her at all. We did that shot six, seven, eight hundred times. We just kept shooting it over and over and over.

Did she give you something that fed you or helped you in the scene?

Absolutely. That's how it gets done.

Can you describe what she gave you?

She was totally in it. She was totally believable. She was totally present. I knew that the world knew that I had her so tightly by the throat that she could hardly breathe. She feared desperately for her life and believed that I absolutely would stick that scissors in and pluck out one of her eyes. That makes you look good.

You had something to do with it, too.
Of course. I'm there. I'm offering the threat in as meaningful a way as she is responding to it. One is adding to the other. You read power to power.

It was most frightening when you told her to choose which eye she wanted you to remove. And then you took the scissors and in a playful/sadistic way pretended they were a pair of eyeglasses.
Again that comes from working with someone who is fully there. It works, there was something emotional, an electricity.

Glory **was a whole different role for you.**
Glory was a labor of love. I was working with an entire group of people who saw it in the same light—a story that was way overdue. And everyone had the desire to do the absolute best we possibly could. Also having a production staff, a director, producer—all these people who know what they want and yet they are receptive to my input.

How important is that to you—that you have a certain input?
Very important. It makes an incredible difference. I can't stand to work with people who are not receptive to my input.

What about the part attracted you?
It wasn't the part that attracted me at all. It was the story itself. I would have done any role. I just wanted to be in it.

You've also said you wanted to do a black Western. Why?
Well, if you think about it, it's because blacks have been completely eliminated from the West. People act like none ever lived there or that no black ever crossed the Mississippi River. And in fact, one out of every three cowboys was black or Mexican. That's one bit of statistics. In different parts of the country the ratio was different. But there were an incredible number of black cowboys—from early on.

So you would do the first real black Western?
Right. But the thing about the movies is that if a moviemaker started out being black there would be no whites in the movies. It's just the way it's done. If you write a book you're not going to write about Chinese. Unless you see some Chinese story and you're able to do research, but primarily you're gonna write about whites. There are exceptions, like the Gershwins with *Porgy and Bess*.

Do you want to write the Western in addition to acting in it?
No, I don't write. I do sit down to my word processor and bang out ideas. But I've come to the conclusion that writing is not one of my talents. I've always liked reading good writing, but I don't write.

Is directing something you've considered doing?
Oh yeah, I like directing and I'm very good at that.

How did you get into acting?
I was always an actor. I was always good at pretending. I always played full-out, you know. I think that's all I do now.

You started very young, didn't you?
Yeah, when I was around eight. But I don't know if my childhood affected my acting at all. Your childhood is your childhood. Your ups and downs are your ups and downs.

You had quite a few of those in later years when you were trying to get work in New York and Hollywood.
Yeah. The typical type of actor's struggle. Part of it was fate and part of it was just an incredible number of friends who just thought I ought to be doing this.

You have four kids and a few grandkids. Was it hard having a family and being an actor as well?
I didn't have a family.

You mean you didn't raise them?
Right.

Did that make it easier to devote yourself to your work?

I didn't have a choice. I just had to.

What about your wife? Is she in the business as well?
Yes, she's a costume designer.

How did she deal with the ups and downs?
She's a coper.

What was the toughest time?
A couple of years in '81 or '82, when I was just unemployable. And I was in my 40s when it happened.

You say you dealt with it through friends and drive...
In that situation I didn't know how to deal with it. The first year you know sooner or later the phone's gonna ring. The second year you begin to realize it doesn't have to. And then also you start to think, "OK, what am I going to do? I better go out and maybe try and get a hack license. I'm not a businessman. I can't go into business. I don't do that well at all."

So what kept you going?
I don't know. You don't cut your wrists. At least I don't. You find something else.

What did you find?
A boat. I've had it since I was 35. As long as I've got a boat it really doesn't matter.

You mean your sailboat. What about it do you love?
I don't know. I always wanted to fly. Getting in a plane turned out to be not my idea of flying. Then I discovered sailboats. And there it was—wings.

On the water.
Right.

Does it do the same thing for you as acting?
I guess it does. It does fulfill me.

What drew you to do the movie based on the high school principal, Joe Clarke?

I thought he was a man who was great. He believed strongly in what he was doing. And I believed strongly in what he was doing. I find myself sighing that it didn't work out as well as it could have or should have—or maybe it did. Sometimes you don't know. Things always happen as they should, I guess.

Wasn't Clarke often on location when you were shooting?
Yeah, and if he hadn't been around I never would have been able to do it. Because I never would have been able to figure out who, why and what. But to be around him, to study him and feel him, his energy and the power that drove him, was a great help to me.

And that's a whole different type of acting when you're portraying someone who is...
Alive and looking over your shoulder.

Was that frightening or exciting?
Both.

Pauline Kael—referring to *Streetsmart*—called you "the best actor in America." How did that make you feel?
Well, it's just a compliment. You take it and let it go.

> When you play the situation, not the result, you're very strong and it doesn't matter what people say.

ANNE JACKSON
Actress

> After a couple of movies I'm eager to find a play to go back to, so that I can have my moment on stage where you say, 'Oh my God, look at his response to that.'

ELI WALLACH
Actor

Amid a myriad of clocks in their upper West Side apartment in Manhattan, Anne Jackson and Eli Wallach talked about their marriage and their work together in careers spanning four decades. They have acted together in 15 plays, several films and many TV shows.

Jackson and Wallach met when they were cast opposite each other at the Equity Library Theatre in *This Property Is Condemned*, by Tennessee Williams. She played a 13-year-old prostitute. He was supposed to be 15, though he was straight out of the Army. Jackson told the director that Wallach was too old for the part, but her future husband proved otherwise.

Born in Brooklyn, Wallach was encouraged by his parents to be a teacher. In 1938, to his relief, he failed a teaching aptitude exam. He then started studies at the Neighborhood Playhouse in New York. When the Actors Studio was founded in 1948, Wallach was in the core group along with Jackson, Marlon Brando, Kevin McCarthy, Maureen Stapleton, Sidney Lumet and John Forsythe.

When the director Herbert Berghof told Jackson she should be an actress, and she agreed, her father was disappointed because he wanted her to be a biologist. He asked her to leave home. Jackson went to live with her sister, Katherine, and like Wallach, started studying at the Neighborhood Playhouse before joining the Actors Studio.

Despite their parents' negative view of their career paths, both were met with huge success. Jackson won an Obie for her role in *The Typist* and was nominated for Tonys for roles in *Oh, Men! Oh, Women!* and Tennessee Williams's *Summer and Smoke*. Wallach, known for his roles in Williams's plays, won a Tony, Theatre World and Donaldson Award for his part in *The Rose Tattoo*.

Each has different styles both professionally and personally. Wallach collects clocks and is on time; Jackson is late and loses things. But they clearly are each other's greatest support. Disagreements and mini-explosions were apparent in this interview. But moments later they were singing each other's praises.

As the interview ended with Wallach waxing poetic about Jackson, he mentioned that she frequently loses her glasses. Instantly Jackson, who was late for an appointment, cried out: "Where are my glasses?" If the scene had been staged, the timing could not have been better. After a mad search, the missing glasses were found along with two new pairs that had just been

Anne Jackson with a three-year-old future director, Ron Howard, on the set in photo by the late Yul Brynner.

delivered by the mailman. As things calmed down, Jackson and Wallach parted ways, planning to meet later in what seemed a most likely setting—a movie theater.

[Jackson and Wallach moved in and out of the room, taking questions first individually and then together.]

How would you define the process of creativity?

Wallach: A lot of it is by accident, a lot of it is the right forces coalescing at the right time.

What are those forces?
Wallach: Things that your mind has stored away. The value of the Actors Studio and the Method was not how to act, it was how to utilize what you've already stored away, and how to channel it properly into scenes.

What's happened more and more in America is that people are now aware of the financial structures of things. They know what's the number one movie, what the cost of it was. It used to be who did you sleep with? And did you wear the bottoms of your pajamas? Now it's, "That picture cost 48 million dollars, and it hasn't recovered."

Can you talk about how you prepared for a specific role?
Wallach: Well, take *The Magnificent Seven*. I was asked to play a Mexican bandit and I thought, "What am I, a man from the city, going down into Mexico to play a bandit? How do I approach it?" Then I thought, "You always see robbers holding up banks or robbing the train, but what do they do with the money?" So I decided I would be an ostentatious bandit. You know, the kinda guy who displays his clothing and his wealth. So I had them make me red silk shirts, I put two gold teeth in my mouth and I had a silver saddle. I displayed what I did with the money. So that was one answer in the creative process.

What about the movie *Baby Doll*?
Wallach: In that movie I thought, "I'm the manager of a cotton gin in the South. The local people are objecting to the fact that

the big plants are taking away from their livelihood, and one of them decides to burn down the cotton gin that I'm managing." The picture basically deals with the kind of revenge I use on people to find out who did it and why and so on. Kazan was a brilliant director, is a brilliant director. He said, "Listen, I want you to walk down the street of this town and I don't want people to say, 'Oh, there's an actor.'" So I put on a T-shirt and a hat and went for a walk. The man I was playing was Sicilian. I grew up with Italians in Little Italy, Brooklyn. And I understand their courtesies, their vengeance and motives and their attitudes and feelings about people. I've spent a lot of time in Italy in the last 25 years. So I thought I understood that aspect of the man.

Can you talk more about the feeling of wanting revenge?

Wallach: There's a scene in the movie where I turn around from the burning wreckage of the cotton gin, and I look right into the camera and say, "I want to find out who did it and why." I had to pick something private in my life that the audience is unaware of, so that when I turn around and face the camera, they connect my loss of the cotton gin and my anger with the cotton gin with the look on my face—they must see a desire for revenge.

How were you able to do that?

Wallach: Well, there's an exercise called the "Magic If." You think of a situation and you say, "What if?" You see children play the game all the time. They say, "I'm gonna go in there and bake a pie." And there's no bakery and no pie, but they imagine it. Well, as you get older that "what if" gets flattened out, it gets dull. People don't utilize it. However, if you have a technique to shake the ashes in you, then you can be creative. So when I was preparing for *Baby Doll* I said, "What if I came home and found my house burned and my wife raped and my children killed, what would that be like?" And then I turned around and faced the camera. So that's a way of getting the creative juices flowing.

So technique is crucial.

Wallach: Definitely. Creating is like trying to pick up mercury. It splinters. The more intense you are, the more you pursue it, the more it will elude you. So you have to get your instrument tuned up and leave it alone. When artists like Shostakovitch perform, they don't say, "My finger has to go here." They know they just have to play. Barbra Streisand used a little aspect of the Method in the song, "Happy Days Are Here Again" and thought, "What if I sing it just after learning my mother died?" If you alter the circumstances privately, nobody knows, and then you've really got something to work with.

Does the outside world ever affect your work on stage or in a film?
Wallach: Yes. Anne and I were doing a two-character play. We had a fight earlier in the afternoon and I told her to shut up! This added another factor when we got on stage which the audience wasn't aware of. So when she got to her line where she had to say, "You have kind-looking eyes," she could hardly say it that night.

You talked about the "what if" exercise. What are some of the other exercises you do to get the juices flowing?
Wallach: The most important thing you can do as an actor is take any behavior and make it look like it's not acting. That's what Method acting teaches you.

Which is why Kazan asked you to just walk down the street like a regular person.
Wallach: Exactly. But you see, if you ask most actors for a certain behavior, like remembering something, they'll raise their eyes and look at the ceiling. Now I don't know what's on the ceiling, but they're indicating to you the conventional cliche of remembering. The Method says, forget that. You can remember by staring at the other person and saying I remember, and it'll have a dynamic that's alive. It's not a cliche. If you look at an actor and you're not aware that they're acting, they're really creating. Marlon (Brando) was a perfect example of this.

He was at the Actors Studio when you were there, wasn't he?
Wallach: Oh yeah, he was at the Studio at the beginning. But he was a unique, breakthrough type of actor because he'd talk and you'd think: He's not acting, it's really happening right now. I saw him on stage, long before he was in the movies, and he was remarkable. But you see, you have to marry talent with

technique. When you get a fusion of the two, then you do well. A lot of actors imitate. You often go to museums in Europe and you see a person sitting there with a big canvas and they're painting a Goya, or they're sitting in the Prado doing different paintings. And they're saying that artist had the discipline and the insight and the know-how. Maybe if I copy it, some of it will flow into me. And so it goes.

How do you define talent? Philip Glass says he doesn't feel he has talent but that he has made up for it by working hard all his life.

Wallach: Well, you can have talent and still have to work hard. People think the equation is talent equals no work, it's just there. And that's not true. I always feel that talent is never satisfied. It's never set. It's always a curiosity. There's a relationship between age and talent and artistry.

In what sense?

Wallach: Well, if you're really an artist you're always curious. Look at conductors who are still working in their 60s, 70s or 80s. They're still up there pumping away. Athletes go through a terrible thing. In tennis an athlete is numbered. He's number two or number four, number seven. In theater, unfortunately, that almost happens too, in another way. Someone, like Julia Roberts, is hot this year—and two years from now there'll be another 16-year-old they've discovered.

But how you utilize your talent is what's important. When I talk to graduating classes I always say that you must think that what you have to offer is unique. No one else thought of it, no one else did it. You have to have that to ease the pain of rejection that you constantly get. I just read for a film and they said, "Wonderfully done. But we're looking for a man with a smashed nose and he's twice your size." So I say, what am I gonna do? To ease the pain I always say, "It's their loss."

What do you think you have that's unique?

Wallach: Well, mine is a marriage between the characters I play and my own sense of fun, no matter who I'm playing—even when I've played killers. I just finished playing a man in a movie called *Mistress* with Robert De Niro and Danny Aiello. It's a small movie but with an amusing premise. I played one of these

Hollywood types—wealthy with a young mistress. You know, the shirt is open to the belly button and they wear gold chains and they work on their arm muscles. All of that was fun, to create that kind of guy. Before, I played an old Army veteran who'd been stored and warehoused in a hospital.

What was fun about that?
Wallach: Well, I knew the situation. In the Army I was a medic. I spent five years in Army hospitals. I knew what it was like to want to stay in the hospital and not be sent back out into the lines and I knew the machinery of how to do it. And I kept thinking about my attitude toward young doctors in the Army.

What was your attitude?
Wallach: To give you an example, when a young doctor comes in and says, "Good morning. I'm here to examine you," I have a dirty line. I say, "It's a waste of time, kid. I've been examined more times than you got wrinkles on your nuts." That's my first line and I knew it would lead me somewhere. It's like Joe Heller says, "I'm asleep and I wake up and I get the first line of a book. I don't know what the book's about, but that first line pops up." Maybe the first line is something like, "And then he slammed the door, with regret." So Joe Heller begins the story with his first line, which leads into a certain maze. And that's how he writes his book.

So what you're saying is you begin with a line or an idea, like your attitude toward the young doctors in the Army.
Wallach: Right. I leave my instrument alone for an invasion of an inspirational idea or something, but I don't know when it's gonna come. We're gonna see a movie sometime soon. These two young Cohen brothers made this movie called *Barton Fink*. And what they say is this kid is hired to write a screenplay and he sits in front of a typewriter and nothing comes. It's a blank page. Sometimes you just have to wait.

Let's talk about *Nuts*, the film you did with Barbra Streisand.
Wallach: When I was on a ship recently, floating up to Alaska, they showed *Nuts*. Each cabin had a TV set and that's what they were showing. I thought *I'd* go nuts! I had one funny incident with Marty Ritt, who was directing. In the movie I was the

prison psychiatrist and I had to testify first. So I went to him and I said, "Why do I have to sit in the courtroom for the next six weeks while you do Karl Malden?" And he says, "What do you mean? You're getting paid! When I turn the camera on, I want to see you sitting in the courtroom." So after three weeks of sitting there, I went to him and I said, "I'm a prison psychiatrist. I have a lot of other patients and they need me." So he says, "You're not going anywhere. You're gonna sit right in the courtroom."

How did you work on your character?
Wallach: Well, I looked at this man as someone who thought he knew a lot. But when Barbra talked to him face-to-face, the things that she said to him always hit home. He could try and dismiss her by telling himself she's mentally unstable. However, the thing she said is, "You couldn't practice on Park Avenue, you're stuck away in this prison thing. You're down the ladder in the achievements as a psychiatrist, let's face it. Therefore you're trying to establish something which isn't true, which is saying I'm incapable of defending myself." And the more she did that, the more insecure he became. But that had to happen in the scene.

You said he thought he knew a lot.
Wallach: Yes, but he didn't.

Did you see him differently than he saw himself?
Wallach: Yes, in a way. I thought, he seems to be unsympathetic but he doesn't think he's unsympathetic. In the first scene I did with Barbra, my character laughs at her character. I ask her, "Would you like some coffee?" She says, "As long as it doesn't have medicine in it." And I say, "No, just cream and sugar." He really thinks, "I'm doing my best."

I did a movie with Candice Bergen where I played another prison psychiatrist. It was called *Murder by Reason of Insanity*. It was about a Polish lady and her husband who came to America and how she changed. They were both nuclear scientists, but she received greater recognition here than in Poland. That drove him crazy and he threatened to kill her. He said that she was molesting the children. And finally he attacked her. The judge said, "You have to stay away from her," and he said, "I'm gonna kill her, whether I'm in prison or wherever I am, I'm gonna kill her."

So they put him in a psychiatric hospital.

Is this a true story?
Wallach: Yes.

Why did you choose the role of the psychiatrist?
Wallach: Because there was a moment in it where I've given the husband permission to go out. The nurse is horrified, and I say to the nurse, "I've handled many of these cases. Don't worry, I know what I'm doing." The husband leaves and sure enough he kills his wife. And the moment I wanted was when the nurse comes into my office and throws the paper down on the counter and the headline says "So-and-so murdered by husband." I wanted that moment of realizing what I'd done.

Again here is a man who thought he knew more than he did.
Wallach: Right. And he realizes that. That moment is very revealing. It destroys that man in that one second. All his expertise has gone out the window because he made a decision and he was wrong. It's like these guys who just had this coup against Gorbachev and Yeltsin, and now they're fleeing. They're on their way to the airport and they're going to be arrested.

How did that moment play on screen?
Wallach: Unfortunately they cut it. All you see is the nurse throwing down the newspaper and the camera zooming in on the headline. There's no cut to me. In movies the actor has no say over what finally appears on the screen. That's why after a couple of movies I'm eager to find a play to go back to, so that I can have my moment on stage where you say, "Oh my God, look at his response to that."

What were some of your most memorable moments as an actor?
Wallach: A scene from *Camino Royale*. It's one of the great love scenes. It takes place between a young prostitute and Kilroy in a little house of prostitution where he wins the dance award and he says to the little girl, "You don't talk much." She says "You want me to talk?" He says, "That's the way we do it in the States—if you're in the mood for romance." She says, "OK, what do you think of the world monetary situation?"

[Anne Jackson enters]
Wallach: Why don't you talk to Anne now? You'll enjoy that. She's brighter than I am.

[Wallach leaves]

Eli was talking about some of his most memorable roles. What are some of yours?
Jackson: When I played Gertrude [in *Hamlet*]. I once asked Meg Wynn Owen, "How do I play Gertrude and make that believable?" She said, "Annie, (director) Peter Hall gave me the clue to that. He said, 'Play her with lots of rings and a silk handkerchief.'" She said, "Well, think about it, Annie. Think about it." And that's all she would tell me.

Did that help?
Jackson: Not at first, because I thought: lots of rings and a silk handkerchief? That sounds so external. And then I realized that anybody who wears lots of rings and carries a silk handkerchief doesn't blow her nose on the handkerchief, nor does she ever do anything with her hands. That's a queenly thing. Nor would she ever suckle her baby. So I started thinking about those things in realistic terms—very specific things for a fast fix, because I didn't have time to go into greater depth nor did I have to do more than one scene. But even something like perfume on my handkerchief gave me something to believe in, so that I wasn't acting out somebody else's version of a queen. At least she was my queen, whoever she was.

Can you think of any other times where someone suggested something that helped you play a scene?
Jackson: Well, I'm very receptive to help. But I'm such an egotist, it has to be that kind of help that I can fathom out. And a really good director, or somebody who knows how to talk about art, gives you that. Like Marty Fried in *The Diary of Anne Frank*.

What did he tell you?
Jackson: In one scene we had a celebration with a cake. And Marty said the cake that they had has to feed a lot of people but it's only as big as a cupcake. So he had a tiny cake on the stage for the Frank family and the other family, and we had to divide

it up. I can't tell you what that did to all of us when we saw that cake on stage—just presenting that reality on the stage. Fried kept saying, "A tiny cake. I don't want a big cake!" Everyone else thought it was comic to have a small cake on stage. But he insisted. Those things that people find to create a reality are so important.

Have there been times when you used personal moments from your own life to help you create a character?

Jackson: Yes, when I was doing *Cleopatra* at the Actors Studio. I was working with [director] Arthur Storch. I was dealing with jealousy and Storch said, "You do the lines well but what would happen if Eli went off with someone?" I said, "Don't talk to me about Eli!" He said, "No, I'm going to talk to you about Eli. What would happen if Eli went off with someone?" And at that time you know Eli was working with Marilyn Monroe and all my own jealousies were coming up. So I thought about it, and then I went home and I sat in the dark. Vivian Nathan, a wonderful actress, who taught me a lot, told me to do that. And I teach that now. I tell my students to relax and sit in the dark and understand what is going on inside, not what is out there or how am I going to look when I say this.

And sitting in the dark helped you prepare for that role?

Jackson: Yes, I used that and thought of what Arthur Storch said to me about Eli. And then I was able to reach my own inner source. And that's really all you can ask for. I must say I'm sounding as though each time I work the brainstorm comes, but it doesn't. But you try to allow your work to come from an inner source that is well-founded, an emotional logic, really, by following your own instincts and allowing yourself to be informed by the situation of the play. When you play the situation, not the result, you're very strong and it doesn't matter what people say.

Have there been times when you got a lot of criticism for a role in which you thought you did your best work?

Jackson: Yes. I remember when I did *Rhinoceros*. I got a lot of criticism and a lot of raves. And the criticism, for the first time in my life, didn't really bother me, because what I wanted to do was what was recognized by the people who mattered to me. But the others, I said, "It's their right not to like what I do." It's like if Picasso does a face and abstracts it, and people say, "What is that? That's not art." Or he does *Guernica* and doesn't put red in the painting.

You said you did what you wanted to do. What was that?

Jackson: I made a woman into a character that I knew. The director, Joe Anthony, said to me, "I want you to play her like a cheerleader." Well, that image meant one thing to him; it meant something else to me. It meant ego, being body proud and not having too many brains in one's head. It meant being the feminine little kitten and a character that I don't respect in a woman. I want a woman to be proud of her mind, and to be proud of her body, athletically, but not cutesy-wutesy. So I played a cutesy-wutesy lady because I thought a cutesy lady would become a rhinoceros, would go with the crowd, you know, would, if you will, go with Mr. Bush, be a Republican. I mean that's what I thought. Right or wrong.

What specifically did you do in the role?

Jackson: I saw a picture in the paper of a girl kissing a sailor, you know—with the leg up. So I did that gesture from the time I came on the stage. That was my Daisy, and I took a lot of flak for it, but I also got a lot of yeas. The yeas were more important to me than the nays.

Did your director support this action?

Jackson: Yes, I had come up with this gesture in rehearsal. I was just fooling around and I thought the director would take it away. But he said, "I want you to do that gesture when you become the Rhinoceros." So he used what I was doing, and his production supported it. It's easier to talk about the process once you're done.

[Eli returns]

You said your role in *Camino Royale* was one of your favorites? Have there been times when you did parts that you really didn't care for?

Wallach: Yes, but you must compartmentalize your career so that every role that you get isn't a priceless piece of prose. There are times when you get films and you think, "Oh God, why did I do that?"

Such as?

Wallach: Well, there was one called *The People Next Door*, which I did with Julie Harris. I love Julie. But things just didn't work, they didn't gel. I didn't feel I was right for the role. I usually fight and say, "Yes, I can do that. I can play an Arctic explorer, I can play a black man, it doesn't matter." But in this case, some instinct told me, "No no no—it's wrong for you." That's one example. And just recently we finished a play in which we did three weeks of intensive rehearsals. But the author didn't see our viewpoint and wouldn't make any alterations and the play didn't work. So we felt crushed by that.

How do you deal with that?

Wallach: When we enter a project, particularly a play, we don't know what's going to happen. We did a play once called *Twice Around the Park*. The idea came to us after we had returned from a trip to China. We had just heard a lady named Dr. Ruth Westheimer and we thought there was a play there. So we spoke to our friend, Murray Schisgal, who is a playwright, and told him the idea. And he said, "Listen, I wrote about this years before I ever heard about Dr. Ruth!" So then he wrote another one-act play about a guru called Dr. Oliovsky. He put the two of them together and we decided to do them in Syracuse. We rehearsed for a month and played for a month and a half. Then we took the two plays to Washington, to Baltimore, to Wilmington, and then we opened on Broadway. We were ahead of the game but then there was a terrific snowstorm, and no money to advertise, and out we went. It was a hurtful thing. We wanted to do the second play. It was the funniest thing either one of us had ever been in. We tried to do it on TV but we couldn't sell it to Warner's or HBO. So, I don't know, a lot of it has to do with luck or instinct, or where you are at a certain moment.

What has it been like working together?

Jackson: I think it's like dancers or chess players. You learn a game and you begin to know each other's moves and you can afford to be courageous in acting or in a game because you trust that person. You know that the other person can hit back, can go with you, can change, and there's an excitement in that.

Is there any danger in being so familiar with each other?

Wallach: Yes. For example, in one play, Annie kept bringing up certain points and I was impatient. I said, "Let's get on with it! Do the lines, get through it." But the imperfections in the scenes stuck in her craw. It wasn't until after we opened and began playing that I realized she was right. I was wrong to insist that we move on. I had the juicy part. She had a part that caused her pain because it didn't justify any of her actions. I understood that. In *Rhinoceros* she made a certain choice and I said, "Are you gonna do that in the play?" She said, "Yes, I am gonna do that in the play. That's what I feel and I'm gonna do it." Every review of the play talked about that choice.

Anne, was that the choice based on the photo of the sailor?

Jackson: Yes.

Wallach: So I thought, "I'm gonna keep my mouth shut and maybe she should have the right to express herself." After all, she's an actress, she has an ego, she has a drive, she has a technique. It's hers, not mine.

Have there been times where you've done a project together where the characters didn't work well together?

Jackson: Yes, we did *Twentieth Century*. And the audience was disappointed because those two characters don't come together enough in the play.

Wallach: Or the play *Cafe Crown*.

Jackson: It was imbalanced.

Wallach: We loved the play, but Annie had basically one little scene where she came in.

Jackson: There was another time when we did a film with Michael Landon. Michael didn't like his mother, adored his father, and wrote a melodrama. In his film all of the love and all of the sentimentality went to his father. And his mother was the heavy. So when he sent the script to me, I said, "No, I don't want to do it." I had played the heavy and the man comes out the sweet hero, and I didn't want to do it again. And Michael kept saying, "Please do it. This is my mother and father and it means so much to me and I will change the mother's role." But when we did the film the part was still tilted and it still bothered me. So I vowed that I wouldn't get into that position again.

Have you?

Jackson: Yes. And I hate to say this even in front of Eli, but I have found out what a battle women have had to fight. I've learned it the rough way, in seeing all those old films where it would be the man's film and the lady would just be a token. Her part wouldn't even be written, except if she was a big star—then they'd strengthen her part.

How does that affect your relationship with Eli—if he has the bigger role?

Jackson: Or the better role. It's hard. Unfortunately, I don't let things alone. Eli had a rough time with me on that play because I kept saying, "Wait a minute," and I would drive him crazy. It's not his fault. He's a brilliant actor who does his work and he would get impatient with me. And quite rightly so, because I was trying to make a point that the writer did not get.

And then you have to deal with it at home.

Wallach: I remember when we did a play called *Waltz of the Toreadors*.

Jackson: I adored that.

Wallach: She had one tiny scene in it. But it was a strong scene and she adored making this character ...

Jackson: What tiny scene? I had a whole act! I had the second act scene. Are you joking? That's one of the greatest scenes ever written!

Wallach: I'm saying it was a smaller role.

Jackson: Yes, oh yes, except that Mastroianni was offered to do the part that Eli did. It's a brilliant play, and what a playwright! [Jean Anouilh] And Zoe Caldwell, who is one of our great actresses, was going to play the part that I played, which was the wife. And remember what Mastroianni said? He said, "That's the best part in the play. That woman comes in in one scene and wipes the man right off the stage." And so he didn't want to play that type of man!

Wallach: I want to show you an old program we have. Anne wrote an article in it called "After the Kiss." It deals with us being on the road with *Twice Around the Park*. It's a marvelous article, it's a brilliant article and I think it will answer all the questions about how we work together and what happens in the working process.

Jackson: I'm so thrilled that you liked the article.

Eli mentioned that you were working on *The Typist* and that you had had an argument that afternoon. And that affected your work.

Jackson: Yes, but knowing each other so well can also help your work. Recently we performed in front of a group of psychiatrists. Eli did Lear and I did Cordelia. And I think we never could have done what we did that evening, if we hadn't had such a strong relationship. Eli's reading from a prompter as he's crying over my supposedly dead body. I was so proud of him, that he attempted to do King Lear in four days, without a real rehearsal because there was nobody to direct him. It was as if he went into the eye of the hurricane.

Wallach: I had a problem, because I was too far away from the TelePrompTer, so I had to memorize my role.

Jackson: And at that time Eli only had peripheral vision in one eye. I kept thinking, I don't believe I'm on the stage with this man doing what he's doing, and he was wonderful.

Wallach: Well, we'll see when we get the tape back.

Jackson: No, I know. I know what I feel inside.

Wallach: I want you to read Anne's article because in it she captures what actors go through.

Which is what?

Wallach: A certain pain and anguish. Actors are on an active current when they're in a play, that other people don't understand. You might think they're doing the same thing every night. Well, they're not. The actors are living a life that's turned up three notches on the scale.

Jackson: And anything can happen.

Does that then turn up your own personal life three notches?

Wallach: Well, yes, because you feel—well, say you're playing a gangster. Do you go home and still act like a gangster? No. But you feel fruitful and creative and then your life is richer, that's all.

What qualities do you each have that helps the other one on stage?

Jackson: Eli has a lovely innocence, and it's so infectious in a way. It's as if he's a little boy roaming around into new territory. He doesn't make decisions about how he's going to do something. Sometimes he does, sometimes he gets into what I think are posing positions, but he breaks them himself. I'm impatient with that. I learned from Geraldine Page. She broke every rule of staging there was to break. She just knew how to do that. There was no audience as far as she was concerned. She never came down front and stood and put her face out front, but when it needed to be seen, it was seen. She was just a genius at that. When I worked with her, I caught on very quickly to that thing that she had, so that I never felt upstaged by her.

What about with Eli? Have you ever felt upstaged by him?

Jackson: Yes, I think so. But once we get into the characters and once we get deeply rooted in the play, you forget all that. But it's very hard for the actor not to feel positioned or in the wrong position. It was interesting to work with Mike Nichols because he let the actors do the staging, so that they almost automatically went into the right positions. But when we did a play called *Nest of the Wood Grouse* with Joe Papp, who is a great producer but not a great director, we had very young kids on stage. And he let them loose with the professionals. It was murder because they didn't know how to stage themselves and we had to battle it out. But Eli and I don't have that kind of ego problem. The ego problem I have is that I am a stickler in a scene.

And he's not?

Jackson: No, he's willing to keep going. He's much much easier to work with than I am, I think.

You get obsessive, is that it?

Jackson: I guess obsessive would be a good word. I'm like a little mad animal.

And he's looser about the process?

Jackson: Yes. Yes. I hope that I've gotten mellower and learned somewhat from him. But when I feel that I'm being led by a chain, I get rebellious.

Has there been any competition between the two of you?

Jackson: Yes, I guess there would be. If the character that I'm playing is put in the position of being a heavy, then I get competitive. I say wait a minute! I don't call it competition, I think that it's more a sense of trying to find the right motivation for the character, so that it doesn't get into that cliched type of acting.

Eli, what qualities do you like about Anne that help you on stage?

Wallach: I'll tell you what I love about Anne is her insight, her awareness of the problems in the play or in the character, and how she sets about to solve it. It takes a longer time. We work differently. I tend to want to memorize my part right away and then fool around with colors and so on. But she says, "I don't know how you do that. I want to know why I'm saying what I'm saying before I say it."

Jackson: I truly can say that Eli's way is better because it frees you. If you have the lines down it frees you and the other actor. You're not holding up the other actor. The other way is very self-ish.

Wallach: I don't think of it in terms of being selfish. I think you felt you couldn't know what stresses or accents to put on the lines unless you knew what you were doing. But in the early days of the theater, when you got your script, you didn't get a complete script. You got the last four words of the other speaker. And that made you damn sure to listen to what the other person said.

Jackson: (Laughing) Just for the last four words.

Wallach: But you began to listen. And then you'd think, "Oh my God, when are those last four words coming?"

You were saying how you loved Anne's insight and awareness of the problems in a play.

Wallach: Yes. I wrote something about her for the actor Roddy McDowell. He's also a wonderful photographer and he has a series of books with pictures of well-known people. And then he asks other people to write about them. His second book is called *Double Exposure* and in it I wrote about Richard Dreyfuss. Anne wrote about Burgess Meredith. Now he has a third book coming out which contains a picture of each of us and he asked us to write about each other. So here's what I wrote about Anne before

I saw the picture he used:

> One picture is worth a thousand words, so it is said. My knowledge of the lady in question is made up of a thousand pictures which I'll try to put into words. She cries aloud in theaters. Talks back to the movie screen. Loses 10 pairs of eyeglasses annually. Mentally tears down ugly office buildings in New York. Dreams of directing traffic, issuing summonses and parking tickets. I give her watches but she's never on time. She always surprises me. She never went to college but has a doctor's degree. Can't carry a tune, but she's musical. Her timing on stage is as perfect as a Movado watch. I love her.

Jackson: He writes beautifully.

How many years have you been working together?
Wallach: Forty-some-odd years.

And do you still feel you have very different styles of acting? Or has that changed?
Wallach: I think I'm slowly coming around to Anne's way in some ways, and she's beginning to adopt some of my ways. Maybe there's something in both of us which will coalesce and make a complete picture.

> Any idea, when reduced to its simplest form, is trite. It's the specifics which are exciting. Art is made of details . . . You may have a story about a man who saves the world, and on the surface it's trite. But through the details you may have something that's electrifying.

NICHOLAS KAZAN
Screenwriter

Nicholas Kazan sits on his porch on a warm summer day, seemingly the guy next door in an unpretentious Santa Monica neighborhood—40-something, dressed casually, his children playing in the kitchen. But when Kazan begins talking about his writing, another side emerges: intense, introspective, occasionally almost ponderous.

Known for scripting such films as *Reversal of Fortune* (for which he was nominated for an Academy Award) with Jeremy Irons, Ron Silver and Glenn Close, *Frances* with Jessica Lange and Sam Shepard, and *At Close Range* with Sean Penn and Christopher Walken, Kazan is attracted to the dark and mysterious side of his characters.

Kazan himself deploys a certain mysteriousness. At one moment he is revealing; the next he is quite secretive. The tape recorder must be turned off several times as he goes off the record. Certain questions evoke a strange smile on his face, others summon a rather pained expression. One can almost hear, at times, an inner dialogue.

When asked about his father, the legendary director Elia Kazan, Nick closes up immediately. Elia Kazan's image is among those in a hallway photo montage. But Nick has worked very hard not to be cast in his father's shadow.

The younger Kazan's track record suggests he has achieved that goal.

What are some things that helped shape your creativity?

The most important thing was when I had this art teacher in second, third and fourth grade and I would draw these big, flowered comical faces. The art class went all the way through eighth grade, and I continued to draw these rather childish faces. I was embarrassed by it because all my friends were doing detailed, representational work with things in proper scale. My paintings looked like they were being done by a third-grader.

What did your art teacher say?

She said, "That's wonderful, do another one." And I just kept doing them and I thought she was just humoring me. But she was obviously crazy and therefore not prone to humoring any-one. Her enthusiasm was genuine. I didn't understand the basis of it, but I would just do what I wanted because she gave me the feeling that whatever I was doing was all right. And to me, the basis of creativity is having a loose sphincter. You have to be willing to fail—or almost wanting to put yourself in a position where failure seems likely. I don't mean that you don't have a positive outlook; but if everybody thinks something is impossi-ble, why not try it?

So you challenge yourself?

Exactly. Because you know, many of the things we take for granted were once termed impossible. I lived briefly in Colorado Springs, and I learned that Pike's Peak was named after a man who came across the country in the dead of winter and looked up and said, "Man will never climb that peak." And they now run a race up it in the summer.

Were there any other experiences that affected you like that?

Yes. I had another important experience when I was in college. I went to see a play one night, and I came home the next day and a line of dialogue was running in my ear and then a line answer-ing it, and then another line from the first character again. I didn't know who these characters were, I just heard them.

So I went to the typewriter and I wrote down the first line and the second and the third and fourth. I got up an hour and a half later, and I'd written 10 single-spaced pages of this play [*Ballgame*]. I went to my roommate and said, "Look what I did, I just wrote something." After lunch I rewrote it. And subsequently it was performed in college and then professionally. It was sort of automatic writing.

Meaning what?
I had no idea, at first, what I'd written. I gradually discovered who the characters were. And I think my best writing experiences are of that nature, when I don't know I'm there and yet there's a process happening. B.F. Skinner wrote this great thing on "having a poem" where he said, "If I deserve any credit at all it's for serving as a location in which certain processes can take place."

You were like a secretary taking dictation for the characters.
Exactly. In fact I very often have that experience. And then, what's beyond that, is when I'm not even aware of myself. When my work is burning hot, it's pure process. Although I am writing down what's happening, I'm not even aware of myself. I would more liken it to religious dancers who dance for hours and then get in this other state.

Like a trance. What do you do to get into that state?
Well, you can't enter that state if you're distracted. You have to eliminate distractions and not be interrupted by phone calls. Also, if you're doing what you think you're supposed to do, you probably won't get there.

Meaning?
Well, if you're thinking "This character *has* to be a middle-aged professor from Harvard who's got a limp and speaks with a lisp," all of a sudden you've put so many constraints on yourself. Whereas if you just say, "This character is *supposed* to be a middle-aged professor who went to Harvard with a limp," you're more open. Then you ask yourself, "Okay, the door opens. Who walks through?" More often than not, the character who walks through won't be precisely who he's supposed to be, although you're aware of what he's supposed to be and what

he's supposed to accomplish. That is, he has to lecture to someone or murder someone or seduce someone in some strange way. He can still do whatever he's supposed to do but you've accomplished it by turning the situation on its head.

Do you approach your writing this way when you first draft a story?

No. Often I find that my first impulse is to follow the cliche. And cliches are cliches for a reason. They don't get to be cliches by being false. But once I've written a scene which accomplishes what needs to be accomplished in the straightforward cliched fashion, then often I can say, "This scene is really boring. What can I do to stand it on its head?" I know what needs to be done, I've seen how it can be done, now let me do it in a different way.

Can you give specific examples of when that happened?

I wrote a screenplay—that wasn't produced—about the Haitian revolution, and one of the characters was a cab driver. He was based on a real cab driver who shepherded me and the other people involved around Port au Prince. He was kind of an outgoing, enthusiastic person. And when the protagonist arrived, the cab driver said, "I didn't recognize you, you're so good-looking." In a way that was an insult. He'd obviously heard the guy wasn't good-looking, but he said it in such an enthusiastic way that it was charming. But I realized there was something missing from his character and from my whole portrait of the people there, who are extremely mysterious and provocative. They're like jazz music in some way.

So how did you find that missing link?

I realized that I simply had to change the effect of this character from someone who was very enthusiastic to somebody who was very downbeat. Then everything he said would knock you slightly off balance. He was still a warm person, but he was someone who had been filtered through the maze of Haiti. I realized if I altered this, it would add another spark of life to the whole thing.

Can you talk about your work on *Frances*?

I rewrote Frances. The writers before me wrote 10 or 12 drafts. I felt sorry for them because they shouldn't have been put through so many drafts. They did very good work, but they were basically exhausted by the time I was brought in. There was one scene I wrote, when Frances comes down the stairs and tells her mother she doesn't love her anymore. And it was a very powerful and emotional scene, I thought. But it was a hard scene to write, and after writing many versions I still couldn't get to where I needed to be emotionally. I was working until late at night because I was brought in just shortly before they began to shoot. Then one night, around 11 o'clock, I realized that the exhausted, kind of frazzled emotional state I was in might be a good state to write this scene. And indeed it was. My own defenses were down, so my writing could come out in an uninhibited way.

What about *Reversal of Fortune*?

That movie was about a legal appeal, and a legal appeal is not intrinsically dramatic. It's a hundred-odd pieces of paper sent to judges and then there's a half-hour where the lawyer speaks before the judge and then the decision is handed down months later. It's not like a courtroom trial, which is dramatic by its nature. An appeal is based on a case which has already been decided.

So what do you convey to the audience, particularly in a case like this where a good part of the audience knows the story? You don't want to bore those people and you don't want to leave uninformed the people who know nothing about it. So I had a terrible problem.

How did you deal with it?

I had to sort of summarize the case at the beginning. And the producer had mentioned to me jokingly several times that Brian DePalma said he would only do the film if it was about Sunny or Sunny was the hero. And I said, "Wait a minute, maybe this is the solution." So I started to write little snippets that she could say all the way through the film. And if I had been forced to start at page one and begin, I never would have done that. It was in that exploratory phase where I could try anything, that gave me permission to try this idea. In all probability it wasn't going to work. But it did.

So you liberated yourself by not starting at the beginning.

Yes. In fact, I started at the end. When they approached me about writing it, the first scene I wrote was the last scene, when Claus comes in the drugstore and asks for insulin—and then he says, "Just kidding." It felt like a sign.

So you write as ideas and visions come to you.

Well, I write notes all over the place. In my office. Or if an idea comes to me as I'm going to bed, I'll jot it down on a piece of paper. But when I say I write notes, I don't do all these things with cards that other people do. I just write notes—about the characters, lines of dialogue. I do write outlines, but I'll suddenly get excited about a scene partway through and I'll write most of the scene. So I follow my unconscious in dealing with the various problems. And then if there's one thing that I can't figure out, I'll keep coming back to that. And I'll let my imagination go where it leads me.

Some people feel you should write chronologically. But the problem then is that you're not responding to your unconscious impulses.

Sure, you've got to grab it or it'll be gone. And certainly I've had the experience of things being gone. Sometimes I'll write something down and then I'll lose it and I'll have this terrible feeling that I've lost something valuable. Then I'll find the piece of paper later and it seems to have virtually nothing on it. Or sometimes I'll wake up and have these brainstorms and later they'll seem trivial, but I don't believe that's really the case. I believe that if you have a brainstorm and you jot down some sign for yourself, when you see the note in the morning you are able to fill in the specifics of the brainstorm and to follow that path.

Do you believe the specifics of an idea are very important?

Definitely. Any idea, when reduced to its simplest form, is trite. It's the specifics which are exciting. Art is made of details. You need a grand conception, and you have to be excited by that conception. But the excitement is a function of your own neuroses, of what your unconscious—or what the universal unconscious—thinks is important at that moment. You may have a story about a man who saves the world, and on the surface it's trite. But through the details you may have something that's electrifying.

You said you may lose the idea if you don't jot it down.

Yes, because as I said, you're a receptor so you must be available to receive or in all likelihood it won't come again. Some ideas do come back. Sometimes you remember months later that you had this idea, but then it's something which stuck to you. But some things don't stick. It's like dreams. I don't remember my dreams, so I have to write them down.

Do you ever tape record them?

I used to when I was in analysis because it was the only way I could remember them. I would wake up in the middle of the night, realize I had a dream, keep my eyes closed, and I would tape record it. And when I'd wake up, it would be the same experience I'd have writing. I'd wake up, see the tape recorder there and I would say, "Oh yeah, I had a dream last night." But I wouldn't have the faintest idea what the dream was, even though I'd spoken it aloud. And if my writing's going really well, I can get up after having written something and not know anything about what I've written.

Because it stays somewhere in the unconscious?

Right. And what is most difficult is to take what comes from your unconscious and mold it. Sometimes it needs very little work. And then you're blessed. But often it comes in an imperfect form. So what you've done is express something from your unconscious or the collective unconscious, and the germ of what you're trying to express, or the primal energy that you're expressing is valid, but the details are, if not invalid, at least awkward. And you then have to find a way to smooth things out.

Which could cause problems.

Right. It's extremely tricky because often if you change things to make sense, then you lose the power. That's one of the problems in my profession, where people are always trying to take care of logistical problems and logical inconsistencies in screenplays.

Do you feel the inconsistencies are better left unfixed?

Somebody recently told me about a theory called the icebox theory. If the audience isn't bothered about it until they get home and open the icebox for something to eat, then you're OK. There are many movies that work well, but when you start thinking about them you're bothered by some inconsistency. But the fact is, whatever mythic material the film is expressing, or however they're entertaining you, you're carried along by the moment and then what's being expressed is valid.

If you use only realistic logic, you might lose your artistic vision—as with Sunny in *Reversal of Fortune*. Why is there a smile on your face?

I was thinking about a script I worked on once. I was supposed to direct it, but it never happened. It's a comic version of *Oedipus*. It's about a kid who sleeps with his stepmother and kills his father and lives happily ever after. It's actually very funny. I was working with these two producers, and they had some suggestions for how to revise it. But it didn't need any revision. And I rather foolishly said to them, "Look, some of this stuff sort of springs whole from my unconscious and I just couldn't change it. And some of it is connective tissue. And I just did the best I could with it. If you want, I'll go through the script with you scene by scene to show you what can be changed."

Did they agree to that?

Yes. We went through the script page by page, scene by scene. But by the end of this process I didn't want to work with these producers anymore, and I didn't want to think about the script for some time. It was not that I was wrong about my initial statement; I was right. But in analyzing what I'd done, the whole force of what was unconsciously being expressed in that material got bogged down into the literal world. It was as if it wasn't art anymore, it was something that could be changed. And it was a wonderful script and it shouldn't have been changed.

Do you feel art is something that can't be changed? Or perhaps there's an unconscious story already written—which, as a writer, you discover and reveal.

That's right. I try to structure things as best I can before I write them, but often after I've written them I say, "Okay, what's this about?" What's the thematic material, what's my unconscious material? How can I make all that stronger, so that my analytic abilities come into play? But basically what you're doing is trying to reveal that raw material.

That's the hardest part of creativity—trying not to muck it up.
Trying not to muck it up is the hardest part. You can't tamper with it.

You were talking before about being the receptacle for your art. But does your personal life ever get in the way?
Well, it's a terrible problem. The ideal thing for an artist is not to have a family. But the ultimate thing for an artist is not to have anything to do with other people. But if you have nothing to do with people you have no art and you're miserable and you commit suicide. So there has to be a balance. You do have to interact with people. You need the comfort, solace and stimulation of other people and so you just balance it out and you try to have periods where you work more intensively and then periods where you work less intensively and you give more to the people you love.

Have there been times when an idea came to you but you couldn't give it your full attention because of your personal life?
That doesn't happen to me. What happens to me is simply that I would write more, there would be more projects that I could do. If I have an inspiration, it doesn't matter what time of day or night, I'll go and write it down, and if it bears further work, I'll work on it. I've been fortunate enough to be a sought-after screenwriter for a number of years, so I get approached to write a great number of things. Scripts choose me.

Meaning?
If I get approached about something and don't think about it while I'm driving home, I'll turn the project down. But if I start writing notes about a project and the next day I write some more and I continue to write and then after a while I can't stop writing—then I know it's something I have to do. So the project has chosen me. In a certain way it's a passive approach.

You're very connected to deeper, unconscious choices.
Exactly. It's sort of like being a receptor. Being a receptor is a passive thing, but it's also the most active thing because you're actively communicating with something beyond yourself or at least that's the experience you have.

How did *Frances* choose you?
They were about to shoot the film, but they needed some work done, so they sent me the script. I liked the script, which I felt was about somebody who told the truth and got punished for it. And I was attracted and felt an affinity to the character and to what I thought that Jessica Lange could do with the character.

Can you talk more about the idea of getting punished for telling the truth?
I don't think people like it when other people tell the truth all the time. Just like people often don't like it when someone's happy all the time. The times in my life when I felt I was most alive often upset the people around me. I think I was obnoxious to other people and they preferred me when I was more quiet and contemplative. I was once walking down the street in New York City with my college girlfriend and we were wildly happy. And this rather overweight woman stuck out her hand with the fingers pointing, and jabbed me right by my Adam's apple and walked on. I just stood there stunned.

Why do you think she did that?
She didn't want to see people who were happy. It's the same thing with the truth. You can tell the truth sometimes but not all the time. And certainly not the wrong time, certainly not in an awkward way, and certainly not in a way that would inadvertently hurt someone's feelings. And to a certain extent the truth is an absolute. Once you're committed to it . . .

What happens?
Once you're committed to it you can't stop. It's an all-or-nothing proposition, which is what *Frances* was about for me.

What appealed to you about *Reversal of Fortune*?
I really don't know. Alan Dershowitz [von Bulow's lawyer]

was this Jewish guy from Brooklyn, just like some of my closest friends are. And since I felt I knew this guy I thought it would be fun to write. But as it turned out Alan was quite different from my friends and was not the character I thought he was going to be, and Claus turned out to be a delight to write. But it was a very difficult script.

Why?
Because there was so much legal material to go through, and I had to research for months and months before I could start to write.

Why did you like writing Claus?
He was mysterious. I kept going back and forth while I was doing the research, thinking this guy's guilty, this guy's innocent, this guy's guilty. And mystery is essential to the best works of art.

Have there been characters who are so unsettling that you can't really write about them?
I don't think so. I can write about anyone, no matter how horrible they are. I like to find the humanity in everyone, which is why people say I like to write about the dark side of human affairs. I believe that everyone's trying to do the best they can with what they're given, what's happened to them in their lives—their families, their parents, their intelligence and so forth.

Even someone who is a psychopath?
Take the father that I wrote about in *At Close Range*. He's a certifiable monster. He murdered his stepson and a bunch of other kids, he tried to murder his own son and killed his own son's girlfriend. And then he went to a prison that was supposedly 90 percent black and he started a Ku Klux Klan unit and set somebody on fire. That guy is out of his fucking mind!

So what redeeming qualities did he have?
I met a guy who was his friend and who was part of his gang and he said he was a great guy. He said he was good to his friends, he was fun to be with. He was supposedly charming and you could see how people would like him. He had his own code and when the code was broken he was a mean sonofabitch.

But that description would probably apply to the heroes in most of our films. If you look at Westerns or modern Clint Eastwood movies or *Rambo*, you say, "Somebody fucked with this guy's family and now he's going to kill 48 people. And they deserved it." How are those movies different from *At Close Range*?

Can you talk about any influence your father has had on you?
Well, I felt like I had some sort of faith that I would be able to be successful as a writer. So that for many years when I wasn't successful, I continued to have faith in myself when nobody else did.

Were you affected by your father's work?
I don't think I was more affected by his work than other people's.

Was he supportive of your work?
I don't want to get into it.

That look in your eyes suggests we're in dangerous territory.
No, it's not dangerous territory. The only thing that's difficult is being seen in terms of him, which is something I've suffered with my whole life and I'm trying to keep to a minimum.

What about your mother—did she influence you?
My mother was a playwright. But she worked more with other writers. The greatest influence she had on me was that she was blocked as a writer. She spent most of her time playing solitaire. She would start something and she would write page one to 40, and then she'd start again and write page one to 17, and then page one to four, and so on. In terms of what we were talking about before, I guess she didn't give herself permission to fail or to write three horrible scenes and express whatever she needed to express and then figure out what to do with those scenes.

Sometimes my first drafts are terrible. But then I just go back and rewrite them. If you're expressing something which is essential to you, you improve it and use your craft.

Did you ever talk to her about your writing?

No, she died before I was writing.

You said her being blocked affected you because ...
It affected me because I felt rightly or wrongly that she had sacrificed her career for my father's career and that had she not had all these distractions and children, she would have been a productive writer. I'm not sure that that's accurate, but that's what I felt. That's the guilt that I bore. And in some way that has made me more receptive to the problems that women have and to the problems that women have as my characters.

What effect has analysis had on your art?
I was concerned, as I guess many people are, that somehow by losing my neuroses I'd lose the fountain of my creativity. I didn't find that to be true at all, though you never know. There's a road not taken. But it did seem that my creative process became clearer. There were no areas that I was afraid to go into, not that I was aware of them before. I guess if you have profound conflicts that you haven't dealt with, you fight those battles at an unconscious level. And then it's taking some of your unconscious energy and some of your conscious energy. You're not able to give yourself to the task because you're preoccupied with some other concern.

Are there characters that you prefer writing about?
I like to write about people with a lot of juice, who have a strong charge. And I like to write about people who use language in odd and unique ways. I like to write about women and I like to write about psychopaths.

Because you think psychopaths have a lot of juice.
No, because I think psychopaths are repositories of the collective disease. They, too, are receptors. They receive the national neuroses and express them.

So in a way they're like artists.
They're like artists in a certain way, yeah.

We have such a disdain for these people and yet actors want to play them and writers want to write about them.
Well, I think it's because if you come into my house and say, "I

just heard this amazing story about a butcher who was cutting meat all day and his wife came home and his daughter said . . ." —then I'm bored. You come in and say, "There's a story about this butcher who cut up his four children and kept them in the freezer for three years and then he started to grind them up and serve them"—then suddenly I can't believe this is happening. This is not just an expression of the disease of our times. It dates back to Shakespeare, Chaucer and so forth. Extreme actions make effective narratives. So these characters, people who break the boundaries of convention, are more dramatic and interesting in a certain way.

What do you think the difference is between an artist and a psychopath?
I used to think, before I was analyzed, that my writing was a kind of therapy, because I wouldn't remember my dreams. Often when I wrote about really grotesque things I would be in the loveliest mood! My own personal analysis of this is that I was completely expressing whatever disease I had inside of me through my art. So the difference is that you start out in the same place, but the artist takes what he receives and expresses it in an artistic form. The psychopath takes what he receives and expresses it by inflicting pain on other people, which is a sin. You have to deal with your problems, which is part of what analysis teaches you to do.

But the idea of being the receptacle is similar in both?
Yeah. I guess the difficult moral question is, when you write about psychopaths are you letting off psychological steam for the populace or are you inciting them to do the same thing? Someone could go out, after seeing the dark comedy I wrote about *Oedipus*, and murder their father, and somehow the blame would be on me. And maybe rightly so, and yet that would be a misapprehension of the thrust of the work of art. It's dangerous with a popular medium. You can do a painting of anything, and no one will accuse you of inciting people to murder. But a movie is different.

Do you have some apprehension about writing about a psychopath and something happening as a result of the movie?
A little apprehension. If it was a manipulative act rather than

a creative act, then I would feel guilty. And if I set out in a calcu-lated fashion to write a film just to make money and I had scant-ily dressed women tortured and murdered, then I would and should feel guilty, because that's not a creative act, that's a crass commercial act of exploitation. But if I wrote about the same thing, as a work of art, to express something about the way that men denigrate women, and if somebody acted out as a result of the film, then I would say that they didn't understand the work of art. And, yes, they may have taken something from the movie; but the movie only fed something that was going to be expressed anyway. That is their sickness and they're responsible for their own actions.

Are there certain actors that you write for? Jessica Lange?

Jessica Lange was already cast when I was brought in. That's the only time that's ever happened to me. I've always written characters as characters, and then, out of my experience as a playwright, I believe there's somebody who can play the part the way you wrote it. And that is the best person for the part and you should try not to cast against type, unless it's a minor char-acter who's poorly written.

What about *Reversal of Fortune*?

I was very fortunate that the movie was well cast. I mean, obviously, casting is everything. If you have the right cast, then it works.

You started out as a playwright, didn't you?

Yeah, and the great and terrifying thing about the theater is that the play is not the same every night. If you see a movie with different audiences, you also see that a movie isn't the same every night. It depends on who's there, what mood they're in, what the national news is, where the stars are, whether the local sports teams won or lost, whether it's a Friday night and every-body got drunk at dinner, and so forth.

All these factors are greatly increased in the theater, because it's a much more symbiotic relationship. And I found the whole thing terrifying. But the last play I wrote, *Blood Moon*, was sort of audience-proof.

In what sense?

Some nights it played to great hilarity and some nights it played very seriously. It was a serious play but had a very dark comic dimension. But it didn't matter whether the play got a lot of laughs or not, it played either way. That was the only play I've ever written that I thought was audience-proof. The terrifying thing for me as a young playwright was that some nights the play would work and sometimes it wouldn't. It was partially because of the actors and their timing and what was going on with their lives. But it depended more on the audience and the size of the house, and whether I had a few people with a fine antenna for a certain kind of comedy or not.

Can you talk about the nuts and bolts of your work day?

I have an office that's a couple of blocks away and I work from about nine to three or four. Sometimes I get so exhausted I fall asleep in the middle of the day and I take a nap. I write notes until I reach a critical mass, until I can't possibly write any more. Then I'm sort of exploding with the story. Researching can be as short as a couple of days to as long as five months.

What about the writing itself?

It's almost always the same. I'll do a draft in 10 days and take a day off and then do another draft in 10 days and take another day off, and do another draft in 10 days. At the end of that period I hope to have a draft that is reasonably good. Then I show it to friends and start to make changes. I have probably 10 or 12 people that I have shown things to over the years.

Do you isolate yourself when you're writing?

I try to. I don't read a lot, or go to the theater or see movies. I try to see friends as little as possible. A little socializing is OK, but I want to work every day so it's pretty all-consuming. You don't want outside stimuli coming in because you're dealing with all this internal stimuli. I exercise after I finish writing and then I usually go to bed early. I try to get a lot of sleep, because I'm tired. It takes a lot of energy because you're creating a new world and it's not easy.

Tennessee Williams supposedly said that writing is the most violent activity he knew of.

Yes, it's active. It's not passive at all. You're sort of like God, you're creating something out of nothing. But you also have to have the attitude of how can I have fun? After I've written a rough draft, I'll come back and look at it and I'll say, "OK, I've got this scene in which a guy meets somebody and he doesn't know that he knew him 20 years earlier and now how can I make this scene more fun? How can I do something that is unexpected?" And then it's like I set this kind of challenge for myself and all of a sudden the character is speaking.

What do you think your strengths and weaknesses are?

When I'm very passionate about something, I can do it reasonably well. But if I'm doing something that uses more technical skills, then it doesn't turn out as well.

It sounds like you have a strong sense of character.

I like people, so that's a help. And I like all my characters. I think when you write something you're expressing yourself. If you write a work of fiction, you express yourself through the voice you choose. When you write something that's in a dramatic form, you are primarily expressed through the characters. And most characters, in toto, express some version of who you are. I'm a very changeable person. I'm very mercurial. My moods change dramatically, and I also write very different things, both dark and light. In each of those instances, if I put all those characters together, then I'm expressing me and my world view, and how I come to terms with it.

What has had a major influence on your life?

Music has had a big effect on me. I don't usually go to concerts, but when I go to hear jazz or classical music, or sometimes dance, I invariably have a creative experience. I'm sitting there, sort of bored, I'm listening to the music, and all of a sudden my mind starts to think of stories I want to tell. And they just come, sometimes two or three or four. Usually I have not anticipated this experience, and I don't have any notepaper. So at intermission I borrow pieces of paper to write down my thoughts.

Is challenging yourself what keeps your own creative juices flowing?

I think so. Every once in a while I meet someone from another profession who seems to have a very creative outlook and I immediately feel a rapport with them. The thing which we seem to have in common is an attitude that work can be fun and that each individual moment is an opportunity. What tends to happen with most people is that they're afraid they're going to do it wrong so they want to find one correct way to do it. It is hard for them to see that there are an infinite number of ways that anything can be done. You have to have enough confidence to know that if all else fails, you can go back and do it by rote, the way it's always been done.

This is why I write my first draft rather quickly. Then I know that I've got it down on paper. Because I have that security, I have room to play and have fun. I enjoy cooking because you never quite want to make something the same way twice. You always want to fiddle around. Sometimes you've taken something which is delicious and made it a disaster; more often, you try something and it works out great.

> 6 You can't enter thinking of your first line. You come on stage and you see the situation and you say, 'Who left the door open?' It has to happen as if you are saying it for the first time. 9

E.G. MARSHALL

Actor

E.G. Marshall is most easily associated with television's classic *The Defenders* or with the 1957 film *Twelve Angry Men*. But his acting skills have graced a remarkably diverse series of productions, from the New York stage premiere of Samuel Beckett's *Waiting for Godot* with Bert Lahr to Woody Allen's *Interiors*.

The Minnesota native began acting in 1932. In 1933 he joined the Oxford Players, which specialized in classics. His New York debut came in 1938 in the WPA's *Prologue to Glory*. And in 1942 he made his Broadway debut in Samson Raphaelson's *Jason*.

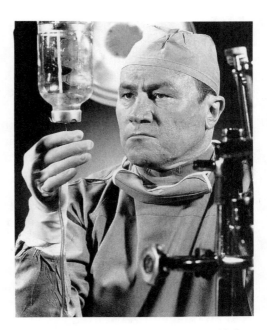

In NBC's *The Bold Ones*: "I try to think what will help the other actor, so it's nice when I get that back."

75

Marshall tired of character roles and continuous typecasting as "the funny little man who comes in with a bucket of beer." His turning point came when he did *The Iceman Cometh* in 1946. It also was the beginning of a close relationship with Eugene O'Neill, whom Marshall considers his mentor.

In 1961, *The Defenders* presented Marshall with the role that made him familiar to everyone. Thirty years later, as a dapper 76-year-old in a sports jacket and slacks, he was still difficult to separate from that courtroom classic.

He was interviewed in a small New York theater—the perfect environment, for he seemed to take in everything in the room within a moment as if he were about to perform. Which, in a way, he did in a two-hour discussion of creativity on stage or before a camera.

In *Twelve Angry Men* there's a line about your character sweating.

Yeah. Jack Klugman says to me, "Don't you ever sweat?"

And at the end you finally do. Do you relate to that character? Or are you a sweater?

No, I'm not a sweater. If I'm working in the garden and it's a hot day, I sweat. But just like that character I don't sweat from mental or emotional stress. That's not to say I don't ponder choices deeply.

What about the choices you make as an actor? How do you choose a play, and how do you prepare for it?

I read the script and I get a kind of feeling about it, an image about it. Then I go back to see if I can be more specific. And then I say yes or no.

You've said that when you were in *Waiting for Godot* you used an image to get started.

Yes. I saw two clowns in a space; and then they act out what's in their imagination. They're in this terrible situation, so they play games to see if they can get that terrible image out of their minds. But it keeps coming back. Who is it? Why does it come back? So then they play another game just to keep life going. To keep the mind going. And then that image comes back again.

What is it?

It's whatever it reminds you of. And I'm not going to tell you what it reminds me of. You've got to make up your own mind. Was it God? "You tell me"—that's what Beckett said.

Weren't you in the play's first New York production?

Yes, but what people don't know is that Herbert Berghof had sent me the play years before it was ever produced. I said, "This is so beautiful—who would let us do it?" He offered his studio, but I couldn't do it because I was busy. But eventually Berghof did wind up directing the New York production.

It got mixed responses, right?

Yes. It was very controversial. Some people hated it and others would come back weeping. And then Bert Lahr, who played opposite me, was beginning to act up, doing some of his burlesque shtick. The producer, Mike Myerbeg, thought we were doing fine and wanted to extend the run. But I had signed into a movie and had to leave the cast. The truth is I didn't want to stay because of Bert. He just couldn't hold onto the part. He'd be doing shtick and it disgusted me. So it closed.

What attracted you to the play in the first place?

The language. And the mystery, the ambiguity. The wait.

Getting back to the images you see—do you close your eyes when you see them?

You don't have to close your eyes, you just see it. But sometimes you can see things incorrectly. There was a scene in *The Master Builder* where we were talking about the death of the child and I was supposed to get very emotional about it. But I thought, "This happened 20 years ago. If he gets emotional about it now, that means he's nuts. Or he's trying to manipulate the young lady he's talking to."

So how did you play it?

Without a great deal of emotion. I told Aline Solness, who played the wife, that the child had died. And that was it. And then I started thinking, "These people in Norway lead bleak, dreary lives. So what did they have? Emotions—which would probably explode." So when I did *John Gabriel Borkman*, another

Ibsen play, I enjoyed the emotion, brought it up like a fond memory. And then it would dramatize itself. I may go back to *The Master Builder* some time.

Do you often go back to parts you have played?
Very rarely. Some actors like to take a part and make it their own. There's a phrase we have, "You hear the old music and it's different." I did *The Crucible* twice because Arthur Miller wanted to put in a new scene. And I'd want to do *The Master Builder* differently. On the other hand, there's nothing different I'd want to do with *Godot*.

So if you did *The Master Builder* again you'd play it more emotionally?
Yes. The way we played it was all repressed. To repress something you have to have something to repress. You feel the emotion and then you hold it down. It's that tension that moves the audience. So with *The Master Builder* you can hold it down so long and then it's got to come out.

What was the most difficult role you played?
Reverend Hale in *The Crucible,* because I thought it wasn't well written. I said to Arthur, "This character just sits there. He doesn't disagree. He doesn't debate." And Arthur said, "Because they didn't have any of that then." But finally he wrote a line and it was a dumb line. It was something about, "All souls walk out." But I did it. I thought, "What the hell."

Was *The Iceman Cometh* a turning point for you?
Yeah. When *The Iceman* opened they had a big audition room in the Theatre Guild and there was O'Neill, his wife, Carlotta, and a few others. And they wouldn't let you take the script away. You had to read it right there. So I did. Then I met O'Neill and we became friends right away.

What do you remember about your first talks with him?
I could talk freely with him and he with me. I could ask anything. He'd explain what he felt, and I identified with that.

Did he talk about his writing?
Oh yes. He'd say, "Oh (*The Iceman*) is so long, so dour." And I

think it was opening night—the lights were dim and I was playing the lawyer then. And someone in the audience shouted, "Turn up the lights so we can see that pile of shit on stage." That's a great introduction, isn't it?

What did you do after the play?
Well, he wanted me to play all his parts. We were working on *Desire Under the Elms* and *Mourning Becomes Electra*. But his physical condition was deteriorating, so he returned to Boston.

Did you keep in touch?
Sure. He even said to another writer that I was the best actor in the country—which wasn't true, of course. But I would have played all those parts had he been in better physical condition.

Can you talk a little bit more about how *The Iceman* was a turning point for you?
Well, I had done a lot of funny little parts. But after doing such good theater I learned to say "no" the way O'Neill did, to plays that weren't of the same quality.

So O'Neill was also very selective about his choices.
Yes, and that was in response to his father, who was an actor. He felt his father had ruined his life by doing the same thing— *The Count of Monte Cristo*—over and over again. He used to imitate how his father at the end of his career would say, "I pissed it away. Just for what? For money?" He felt his father could have been a great actor. He could have played *Hamlet*, *Macbeth* and *King Lear*, but he never did because he was making this cushy, easy living repeating his role in *The Count*. So O'Neill determined that he would be very strict about his own career.

Do you have your own Monte Cristo?
TV. I don't mean to look down on TV or movies. But you don't put your name on it. You're just getting your check.

But what about something like *The Defenders*, which received so much acclaim? Did you enjoy doing that show?
Actually it turned out to be three of the happiest years in my life. But, you know, I wasn't the first choice. First there was Fredric March and Ralph Bellamy. They both said no.

What did you like about the show?

Well, it kept me in New York. I hate L.A. And we had good writers and actors on the show. And we introduced subjects like blacklisting, abortion, white-collar crime, race relations.

Did you influence the scripts in any way?

Yes. Reggie Rose, who was the original writer and story editor, was very open. I rewrote a scene with Arthur Hill. Reggie trusted me because he knew I wasn't going to screw it up.

You're very active politically, and *The Defenders* was fairly consistent with your beliefs. But were there roles you wouldn't play because they were contrary to your politics?

A journalist once asked, "How can you play that part?" And I said, "I don't believe in regicide but I played Macbeth." I don't like crooked lawyers or politicians but I would play them. But I wouldn't do propaganda for an ideology that was alien to me or that I didn't approve of.

You've worked with so many different directors. Are there any you work best with—or that you had particular problems with?

Well, I worked with George Roy Hill on a TV show, with Joanne Woodward and Barbara Barrie. And in *The Gang's All Here* George wanted Pat O'Brien for the part. He said to me, "I've never seen you lose control."

I said, "You bet your sweet ass you haven't. The whole point is control." So I had a difficult time with him on the show because he really didn't want me and I wasn't about to take crap from him or any other director.

Meaning what, exactly?

Meaning when I work with a director he has to be honest and open with me and not expect me to do phony stuff just because that's what he has in his mind. It's got to be organic with me. If I can't see it, then you have to explain it to me. Like in Woody Allen's *Interiors*—I wanted to play the scene where I tell Geraldine Page I'm leaving one way, and Woody wanted me to do it another way.

How did you want to do it?

Like I was presenting a very rational way to get ourselves out of the situation, to make it look attractive. But Woody said, "Just tell it. Say, 'I'm leaving and that's it.'" I thought that wasn't dramatic enough, but I did it his way because it was his idea. Ironically, it turned out that Ingmar Bergman praised that scene and praised me for doing it that way. That's why I always say I shouldn't put myself into the part. I should put the part into myself.

How so?
If I were talking to my wife and children in real life, I'd say, "We're not in a very good situation. So why don't we have a separation and then we'll see how it works, OK?" I'd want to soften the blow, but Woody wanted me to present it as a fait accompli. Bergman, the Swede, liked that better. So did Woody. But I didn't want to hurt anybody. Because that's me.

What qualities in a director bring out your most creative side?
Insight into people. What makes people do what they do? Mike Nichols has a way of saying short things like, "Like her a little more. It's not hard."

And that helps?
It does if I'm being too distant. It helps me reach out more. After a rehearsal Mike will say, "Just two little things." So when I was in China, I had a pair of chopsticks made with "Just two little things" in Chinese. The supplier asked "You mean 'two' or 'too' or 'to' little things?" I said, "Just two little things." Later I asked a fellow at the U.S. Embassy what was written on the chopsticks. And he said, "Two little pieces of things."

What did Mike say when you gave them to him?
He said, "I've changed all that. It's, 'Just two little things of great importance.'"

What were the differences between working with someone like Woody Allen and some of the other directors you've worked with?
Once I said to Woody about a line, "That's all so literary." And it never appeared in the picture. But I think you shouldn't be like

a puppet. It shows when you see actors who are doing just what the director said.

Which actors have brought out the best in you?
Maureen Stapleton, Colleen Dewhurst.

Why?
They look at you. You see a real person there. I try to think what will help the other actor, so it's nice when I get that back. The trouble is that many actors want to play by themselves. One time at the Actors Studio, Berghof was saying how he couldn't get Eva Le Gallienne to look at him. Bobby Lewis said, "Just go up on your lines and you'll get more attention than you can handle! Just pause when she's waiting for you to respond. Then she'll look at you."

Who was the most difficult actor to work with?
Bert Lahr. He had this need to do his shtick and that made him very difficult. He was the comic, and I was the straight man, and a straight man isn't supposed to be funny. He walked out on rehearsal once because he thought I was too funny. And on opening night of *Waiting for Godot* I got an enormous laugh on my line, "That passed the time," when it was Bert's line, "It would have passed in any case," that was supposed to get the laugh.

What did he do?
He turned red. But then he got a bigger laugh when he said his line. And I thought, "Thank God." He was terribly competitive. So I had to get him to like me personally. I had to seduce him—have lunch with him, see his family—just be his lover.

So there's a romance to the business of acting.
Yes. Directors court actors, too. I asked a director once, "How the hell did you get that performance out of that guy?"
He said, "I took him to lunch; I bought him ties."

There was a movie you were in with Orson Welles...
Yes, *Compulsion*. He was such a pompous person. And he acted like he was king of the world. At that time he was so deep in debt to the IRS. He should have been easier to work with. He

never wanted you to look at him. There was a scene where he was supposed to be telling me something. So I'm sitting there and he said, "Would you mind not looking at me when I'm talking? I don't want to fight your look." So he's talking and I take my glasses off and put them down, keeping my eyes closed as he goes on and on. He finishes the scene and they say, "Cut." And he says, "You were a good soldier."

Maybe it's your penetrating look that got to him.
Yes, my piercing eyes. But we parted friends. And then I read in an interview that he said, "There are three actors who really think when they're acting: Greta Garbo, Charlie Chaplin and E.G. Marshall."

You talked about being free on stage. How do you do that?
You can't enter thinking of your first line. You come on stage and you see the situation and you say, "Who left the door open?" It has to happen as if you are saying it for the first time.

What do you do to help create that freshness?
I warm my voice up, have some hot tea and make sure I don't have to go to the toilet when I get on stage. And then I clear my mind so I'm not worrying.

Do you identify with the characters you play? Have you ever played a character who was really you?
A character is a different person from yourself. I can't say that I ever played anything that was myself.

Who is that?
Who is me? You'll never find out!

Will you at least say what your initials stand for? You've been mysterious about it.
Do you want to hear it from the horse's mouth? The story goes that "E" stands for "Edda" from the Norse legends and "G" stands for "Gunnar." All Norse kings' names begin with G. So my name was Edda Gunnar Marshall. But when I was in the second grade the teacher called me "Edna" and all the kids laughed at me. I explained this problem to my third-grade teacher, who told the kids my name was Edda, not Edna, and they still

laughed. So the only way to solve this matter was to use my initials, E.G.

So is this the real story?

No, I never tell the truth about this. I also say my name's "Egregious Gregarious Marshall." And when people laugh I say, "I didn't laugh at your name. Why do you think mine is funny?"

Isn't it provocative to have two initials?

What about W.C. Fields, e.e. cummings and A.R. Gurney?

At least with Gurney people also call him Pete. Speaking of whom, didn't you just finish doing his play, *Love Letters*?

Yes, with Colleen Dewhurst. Actually, I'd wanted to buy *Love Letters* when I first heard about it, but I was told it was sold. So later on, when they wanted me to do it in New York, I said, "No." But then they asked if I would do it with Colleen in Boston and I said, "You bet." And we did it.

You said she was a very giving actress.

Yes. She did *Love Letters* like a person who's been through a hell of a lot, and that worked very well against my upper-middle-class waspish attitude about things.

How does it affect you when you don't get a response you expect from the audience?

Some actors say, "What the hell's the matter with them? They're sitting on their hands." I say you keep playing.

And reviews?

I don't read reviews because they have nothing to do with you. If reviewers could write plays they would. They review them instead. And they can't help you.

How do you feel if your director or producer doesn't like your work?

When I was in my first Broadway play, *Jason*, which Samson Raphaelson wrote, I was in my 30s and I was playing a 72-year-old man. After our first run-through, George Abbot, who was producing it, said, "I don't know what you're doing. But it's not funny." Well, it turned out that I was a big hit. Every critic mentioned my small part. I saw Abbott some time after that and he said, "Worked out all right, didn't it?"

So you are able to deal with criticism now?
Yes. You can say something and I'll say, "You have a point there." But I know some actors who can't survive because they can't take criticism.

What do you think is your chief strength as an actor?
My ability to adapt. When I was a boy, my minister wanted me to join the seminary. But I wanted to be an actor. He said, "You're not fit for it. Your voice is thin and you're no Rudolph Valentino." And then I thought, "Does that make me a good minister?" So then I studied voice and speech. I had to equip myself. You may have a God-given gift but you can't handle it unless you have the tools, the technique. If I see something lacking, I try to acquire it or adapt to it.

Is that what being a great character actor is about—to be able to adapt to different kinds of roles?
Yes. You have to put that sort of person in your mind. Why does that person want to do that? Where does it come from? There has to be some motivation for the way the character behaves.

What are your weaknesses?
I played *Macbeth* and I found that physical movement on stage doesn't come easily for me. I've studied fencing, but I'm not good at sports and I never was. I always wanted to be able to ride, so I studied riding in Vienna. I had a marvelous outfit. But there was something missing in me—the coordination.

So you've never done any Westerns?
Actually, I've been in a couple. One was *Broken Lance* with Spencer Tracy. And the other was a remake of the *Oxbow Incident*. I sat on a horse for three days doing close-ups.
Do you know what it's like to sit for three days on a hard saddle?

What do you like most about acting?
Working with good materials and good people. And I've

made money at it. But I don't like doing movies. It's boring. I don't know how anyone can stand making movies. I worked for 12 weeks on one film. We were always waiting around. How can you enjoy that?

What do you do while you're waiting?
I read letters. I collect the letters of Joyce, Ezra Pound, and Michelangelo. I went back to them the other day. In one letter Michelangelo was telling his brother that he didn't like the six shirts he had sent him. And he'd say things like, "Well, I met the bishop. I'm supposed to do this commission. Maybe I'll get a little money for it. I need that money to pay the rent." Or he'd say, "I'm building my house," and he'd describe the plumbing arrangements and so forth.

Then the letters help you get to know these people?
Yes. They're like diaries. You find out what people were doing at the time. It's not from the imagination. Here's this problem, I have these shirts and I don't like them. Also, you learn what living was like, how things were born—how governments were started. While you're waiting around on a movie set, you can read two or 200. I'll read things like the correspondence between James Joyce and Ezra Pound. Or Pound's letters to T.S. Eliot about what to take out of *The Wasteland*.

Is that why you were attracted to *Love Letters*?
Yes.

Are you a letter writer yourself?
Yes. People tell me I shouldn't write letters. But I disagree. I think you can tell more in a letter than you can tell in a telephone conversation.

You've been acting for a long time. How has your work changed?
It gets easier in one way. George Scott and I talked about this. You have your technique and you've learned some things. And what's harder is now that you know more you have to do more.

How has your life affected your art and vice versa?
Kevin McCarthy and I have both done *Love Letters*, and we

were saying how people who have lived do this play better. You bring your understanding of life to your work. When John Gielgud was doing *King Lear*, he was talking to Cordelia and tears came down. Someone said, "Mr. Gielgud, how can you cry every night?" He said, "I have difficulty not crying."

Do you feel that with *Love Letters*?
Yes. I have no difficulty with the emotion; it just comes up. Because of what I've lived, I guess. I think that comes from living, from understanding, from not being too judgmental of other people.

Have there been roles that changed you in some way?
The wonderful language in *Godot* made me think more. And after doing it for a while, I could talk in Beckett's language.

What did it make you think about?
The existentialists. I got very involved in their writing, which gives you a better understanding of yourself and your place in the universe. That sent me off in a different direction.

What about mentors? Have you had any?
I guess you could say O'Neill was a mentor. We had long talks and he had me reading a lot. He even read a series of short plays I wrote called *Ways, Means and Ends*. He said he wished he could write like that. Because my plays were short.

What was the most special thing about O'Neill?
His philosophy: "To thine own self be true." He thought you should be yourself. You should unify, not fragment yourself. He had a tragic vision. He thought optimism and happiness "were the biggest pipe dream of them all." But when he'd talk about tragic things he'd always laugh. His brother James would fall dead drunk down the stairs and he'd laugh talking about that. He had a tragic sense, but he laughed about it.

Is that what you liked? Because you don't seem to have that dark side.
I do have it. I think I just sublimate it. I subvert it.

A quiet dark side.

Like I said this morning, "The ranks are thinning. All my contemporaries are dying." Only four of the actors from *Twelve Angry Men* are alive. And there's Kevin McCarthy. But he's four months older than I am. He should go first. You've got to accept it. Some people say, "Why me?" Well, who else? Who would you rather?

Do you think about your life and your age a great deal?
No, I just can't believe I'm 76. I don't think of the past so much—which is a blessing.

Was there something in particular that O'Neill said that really had an impact on you?
He said, "Don't sell yourself out." But I modified that to say, "Not in the theater." You can do TV and movies, but the theater, that's your religion. That's your church.

Did your family have a big effect on your acting?
A friend and I used to walk down a road in Maryland on the way to a swimming pool. We'd talk about life and girls. And he said, "Aren't you glad you weren't shy when your mother asked you to recite for the folks?" How does it start? No one urged me. My minister tried to discourage me. It was something I wanted to do.

How does it start?
I don't know. It was always there. They asked Shaw, "When did you first want to be a writer?" He said, "I never wanted to be, I always was." And so was I—I was always doing things, rehearsing things.

Has there been a part that you've always wanted to do?
It hasn't been written yet.

What about a play that you see differently now?
There is one—called *Queen After Death*. I did it about 30 years ago. A friend thought it would be perfect for me. So I agreed to do it before I had even read it. And as we rehearsed it, I realized I didn't know what it was about. They wanted me to continue with it and I said, "I really can't and it would be dishonest because I don't know what I'm doing up there." But I recorded

the entire thing and then years afterward I found the tape and I played it.

What was your reaction?
I said, "My God, this is a wonderful play. Why didn't I understand it? I'd like to do it now." So I told the producer, T. Edward Hambleton, and he said, "Well, it's a pity I'm no longer producing plays."

What did you say?
Well, I didn't sweat about it!

> ❝ Most of my creative time happens in noisy places. I can write better at an airport. And I can think more clearly in my car and in a traffic jam than almost anywhere. ❞

SUE MARX
Documentary Filmmaker

Sue Marx loves magic. She loves to watch it and create it. And she has created it more than 40 times as a director and producer of documentary, political and educational films and videos.

Since 1979 Marx, who is from Detroit, has produced and directed such Emmy Award-winning films as *John Voelker (alias Robert Traver)*: *Anatomy of an Author*, a 20-minute portrait of the former Michigan Supreme Court Justice who wrote *Anatomy of a Murder*; *Buffalo Soldier*, an 11-minute dance film revolving around a regi-

Sue Marx: "I keep saying I want to do a feature film and then I think, 'Do you really?'"

ment of black soldiers in the Civil War, with music by Quincy Jones; and *Encore on Woodward*: *Detroit's Fox Theatre*, a 25-minute film about the world's largest movie house, narrated by Bob Hope.

Marx's ability to take the life of a judge or a movie house and turn it into a magical moment on film has won her many national and international awards, including eight Emmys, nine CINE Golden Eagles, numerous American Film Festival awards, and in 1988 an Academy Award for her documentary, *Young at Heart*. Perhaps her most magical work, this film was shown at the prestigious New York Film Festival and was the first independently produced documentary to air on Soviet television.

Young at Heart, Marx's personal favorite, tells the story of two octogenarians, Reva Shwayder and Louis Gothef, who in the middle of a group trip to England, fall in love. They have much more than age in common. Each has suffered great tragedy— Reva has lost her husband and both her children; Lou has lost his wife to Alzheimer's disease.

Both are artists, too, and have learned to deal with their loss through their work. And their differences—he's a traditionalist and portrait painter, she's an abstract painter who favors Rothko—only bring them closer together. As we watch Lou painting Reva's portrait with brush and canvas, another portrait is being created on film by Marx.

It is more than a coincidence that both Lou Gothef's and Sue Marx's talents lie in creating portraits, for they are father and daughter. Importantly, that relationship is never revealed in the film—because *Young at Heart* is more than a story of a man in his 80s who falls in love. It is also an artist's loving depiction of a father who has finally found happiness after years of grief. "After 10 years of dealing with my mother's illness, all the magic was gone," says Marx. "And then I suddenly saw a freedom of spirit in my father."

Lou Gothef's gift for portraiture and for capturing human emotions is evident in his daughter's work. And it was Gothef, during his years as a scenic artist, who introduced Marx to the world of fantasy when she was a child, taking her backstage for closeup views of performers such as Harry Blackstone Sr.

How do you get ideas for your films? Let's start with *Young at Heart*.

Most of my work has been portraits of people—watching and

shadowing them, becoming very personal with them. Sometimes I have to look for ideas, but this story was sitting in my lap.

How so?

Reva and my father had become the center of gossip among a certain group in the city. They were in their 80s, not married and living together. I mean my dad was actually sleeping at her house. Neighbors across the street would see him in his pajamas in the morning. Can you imagine being gossiped about when you're 85? And I thought, God, if all these people are really interested in their love life, there's a story there.

Did you expect it to win the Academy Award?

No. I thought it would be a short, sweet documentary film where people enjoy themselves. And I thought we'd dispel some of the myths about the negative side of aging—which we did. When they were first dating and having such a ball, everyone, including my husband said, "I can't wait till I'm 80 to have so much fun." We see so much that's depressing about aging—those really horrible stories. Then you see a story that's so uplifting, and you say, "Let's tell it." But I never thought in terms of winning an Oscar.

You said you're interested in "doing portraits." Doesn't your father paint portraits?

Yes. And that's probably why I'm so picture-oriented. But I can't draw a line!

So you paint pictures with your films.

Exactly. And if you combine visuals and storytelling, you take it a step further and you have a movie. I started out as a photo-journalist and did stories in the same way. Picture stories.

What interests you about doing portraits?

I like people and I like looking at them in terms of their creative spirit and the way you're probably looking at me. Why do you do what you do? What compels you? What's in your background? And when you sit around asking people questions about themselves you don't have to talk about yourself.

And you don't like talking about yourself?
No, I hate it.

Why?
I just don't think I have as much to say as other people. Many of the people I pick are very articulate. They have a lot to say about their work and about themselves personally.

When you get an idea, does it come to you over a period of time or is there something that triggers it and you go, "Aha!"
It's just "Aha!" Certainly with documentary films. With feature films it's different. I've got the bug to do a feature film, but there hasn't been an "Aha." I've been puzzling out what I want to do in terms of features for a couple of years. A lot of companies and government institutions have hired me to do films for the past five years. Those pay the rent. But between those times are the ideas I generate such as *Young at Heart*. And another film on magic. I love magic. I raised some money to do a documentary film and National Geographic Television put up the rest for their *Explorer* series. It's called *It's Magic*.

What do you like about magic?
I can't tell you. I've been fascinated ever since I was a kid. My dad was in show biz and he used to take me backstage. There was a famous magician—Harry Blackstone—and I used to watch him all the time when I was a little girl.

Do you remember the tricks he did?
Yeah, and now his son is doing them—Harry Blackstone Jr. Actually he's in our film.

What are your favorite tricks?
I love card tricks. And I have not a clue as to how they work. But Harry and his wife were in town this past weekend and a whole gang of us went out to a restaurant. Harry and another magician started doing card tricks. We were just blown away by it. And then we saw him performing Saturday night and he does this masterful job with a vanishing birdcage, dancing handkerchiefs, floating lightbulbs.

And you don't know how any of these things happen?
Right.

Do you like all kinds of magic?
No, I'm not crazy about sawing a body in half.

Don't filmmakers make magic too in a sense—having things appear and disappear?
Yes, exactly. So many things are just magic. They just fall into place. And you don't know how lucky you can be. What I like about documentaries is that they're serendipitous. You look for moments that are so special and then you grab your cameraman and you say, "See that, get it." It's nothing that you could have anticipated. You can hope that these wonderful things would happen but you never know.

What were some of the best moments you've had—the most magical?
I'm doing a film on child care right now, so we're working with a lot of children. At one point, while we were shooting the film, it was Halloween. And for some reason I wanted to see a parade of all the different children. So we put our camera outside, which was something we hadn't planned. It had nothing to do with the film.

Were you looking for anything in particular?
What I wanted was to catch one of the kids who couldn't keep up with the crowd. And sure enough, there was this little dopey person, dressed up as a mouse. He had a little mouse face and little whiskers taped on and he stopped to pick up a weed or something. You can't direct that kind of thing, at least not in documentaries. You can't even expect it. It's just what happens. If you're lucky, you get it on film.

Are there any other magical moments that you can remember?
There's a scene in the art museum in *Young at Heart*, where Reva and my dad were arguing over the paintings. I knew it would be wonderful but I never expected it to be that incredible. I know they fight all the time about what he likes and she likes.

Can you give an example?

When they were in the museum she was raving about a Rothko painting, calling the colors luminous. And his response was, "So what?"

And they weren't self-conscious when they were in the museum?

No, they just talked, totally unaware of our camera. And they had wireless mikes on.

If you can't control magic is there anything you can do to create it?

You sort of have to develop a sixth sense about what you might hope to get in a scene. You prime the pump, so to speak, and hope that your expectations actually happen.

Don't you sometimes manipulate people in your films?

I might manipulate someone to generate a conversation or a remark—but only if I know from my research that the remark rings true so that the person might have said it anyway. Basically you follow that sixth sense and then just hope for the best. Plus you have a cameraman you can rely on to grab those special moments.

In what way is the cameraman important?

Lighting—that's one of the most important things in a film. And a cameraman has to understand that. If you look back at the wedding scene in *Young at Heart*, you'll see how exquisitely it was lit. It was perfect. And our cameraman had no assistance. What was most difficult was capturing those moments when they said their vows. He had to capture their faces and to get the "I do's" and "I don'ts." He had to keep moving around them gracefully. Fortunately his eye and ear were so good.

Reva and your father didn't object to having their wedding taped?

Actually Reva did mind. She said, "I don't want your camera crew here be tripping over things. And I don't want my wedding ruined." And I said, "You're telling me that after we've finally gotten an ending we can't record it? You're killing me!"

That must have worked.

It did. So our cameraman wore a suit and a tie, as did our soundman, who hid in the bushes.

Is there a particular cameraman you like to work with?

There are several that I know I can always count on. Usually I try and work in a small group. It's much less intrusive. I try and find the right synergy. You need a group that works together, that's cohesive.

What are your biggest concerns when you're working on a film?

I worry about things like, are we getting what we're supposed to get? Is everyone doing their job? Does everyone care about the film? Are they motivated enough? Once, when we were shooting the magic show, our cameraman had to leave on the second day. His mother had a stroke. So we brought in someone else at the last minute.

What was he lacking?

He didn't have the eye, and he didn't have the sensitivity. He was only an operator. We were told he was a director of photography, which is what we wanted. But what he did I could have done.

How did that impact on the film?

The stand-up stuff, the street stuff, would have been so much more wonderful. I mean a lot of the situations themselves dictated good stuff no matter who shot it. But our director of photography would have seen what to do. In the docs we do the director of photography has a major responsibility.

What about the writing? Do you do that or do you work with someone else?

Pamela Conn, who's been associated with me for about five years, does much of the writing. I'm stronger at production and direction.

Are there any editors you've worked with who really stand out?

I've worked with three magnificent editors. But far and away I think the finest editor is the one who did *Young at Heart*. He has a good ear, a good eye and a great sense of music and pacing. He made the story happen in a way I never expected it to happen.

And what was that?

I had never anticipated that I could get the audience to believe that Reva and my father could get married at the very end and yet be surprised as well.

How did he avoid that kind of predictability?

He believed there was enough footage shot to tell the story, that people would believe it and that we could take what was shot in Florida the winter before and make people believe it was their honeymoon at the end.

Then it wasn't their honeymoon?

No, we started shooting in February '86, when they were in Florida for the winter. They weren't married yet, they were just living together. Then we used that footage at the end as if it were their honeymoon.

Can you talk more about the editor's role?

I had fully anticipated that the film was going to open with these two people walking into the marriage license bureau. Then I decided it would be a retelling of the story through flashbacks. That's how I saw it. And it would have worked that way, but it would have been a different story. So my editor said, "Why don't we just make it so that people buy into the notion that they got married at the end?"

I bought into it.

But you would have been satisfied if they'd just continued living together.

Yes, but I preferred their getting married. And I really enjoyed it when they went to the license bureau, acting like young newlyweds, and then revealed that they were born in the early 1900s.

Actually, that was one of the worst moments. We had a substitute sound man the day we went to the license bureau and his tape didn't record. He didn't turn the sound on so he missed the first two takes. So what you saw was the third take where the battery was getting run down. But the first was so much more exciting and vital. They were very fresh—nobody had rehearsed. You don't do two and three takes in docs.

But that was still a wonderful moment for me. It felt right and it was a surprise. But now that I know the whole story, I wonder what would have happened to the film if Reva and your father hadn't decided to get married?

Actually I think they got married *because* of the film.

You mean they would have just continued living together if you hadn't made the film?

Possibly. They were courting when we started this film and they were perfectly content just to be living together. But frankly, I think they got caught up in writing a scenario. I think they liked the story and saw the film as a story romance. It was kind of a strange thing—like a story within a story.

Actually there seem to be many stories within stories. You're the filmmaker telling a love story about two older people. And you're also the daughter of the star, with your own story, watching your father fall in love. When I first watched the film I didn't know the two of you were related.

It's funny that you should say that because people usually don't know that. Whenever I speak to an audience about the film I never tell them who I am until after the screening.

Why?

It biases the viewer. They look for things they wouldn't have looked for otherwise. They think back about things in a different way.

What kind of things would they look for?

A lot of people have asked if it's hard to make a film about a family member. Or why did my father let me tell his story? Or if I hadn't been a family member could I have done the film?

Could you have?

I'm not sure. But I don't want that baggage up front, influencing the audience.

How did telling this story affect you?

I think it affected me a great deal. I had watched the pain that my dad had endured all those years with my mother. We shared as best we could but he was the one who dealt with her day to day. Actually the mourning period began with the day we put her in the nursing home, not when she died.

And when he met Reva it must have been a rebirth of sorts.

It was. I saw this man finally finding some happiness. The film was about celebrating that. Now, had I not witnessed all the other stuff before maybe it wouldn't have been such a knockout story. You look at a metamorphosis of a man who—I don't want to say that he was in great agony for 10 years. He wasn't. But it was very difficult. Fortunately, as an artist himself he had a way to withdraw from all that sort of stuff. When things got too tense or too tough he would go and paint.

So the fact that he is your father helped you make such a unique and sensitive film?

I think so. Because I know how terrible and sad his life had been for 10 years. And I saw how excited he became. It was like he was born again. He had become someone I never knew.

In what way?

He had always worked hard. Both my parents worked hard. But they never had the wherewithal to really make it. Then suddenly I saw a freedom of spirit. He was really in love and there were so many possibilities. I thought maybe that's what he was like when he first met my mom.

But you hadn't seen that side of him before?

No. After some 50 years of marriage and more than 10 of those dealing with illness, all the magic was gone.

Can you talk a little more about the different roles you played? You were the daughter and the filmmaker.

I was the stepdaughter, too.

How did you feel about Reva as a stepmother?

I liked her then and I still do. Actually, I originally knew her as an artist around town, before I made the film. I also knew her husband and her family somewhat and I admired her as a feisty dame.

Did you feel like she was replacing your mother?
No, because my mother had been ill for so long that we sort of went separate ways.

Of all the films you've done is *Young at Heart* your favorite?
Yes, it brought me an Academy Award! My second favorite is the first film I ever did. It was a very short film, about 8 1/2 minutes, and it was a portrait of a potter. I didn't know very much about filmmaking, so I hired a cameraman I'd worked with on Channel 4 when I was there. I went to a foundation and asked if they'd give me a grant, and then together we made the movie for $10,000. It had sound effects, but no sync sound. It was all voice-over.

What did you like about the film?
I thought it was charming—real small but charming. It was simply about a potter's work, how he does it. It was very quiet and it's continuing to sell after 11 years. It's like an evergreen; it's a feel-good movie. I love that film.

What is the most difficult thing about filmmaking for you?
You have to be organized and I'm terribly disorganized.

Really? You don't seem to be.
Nobody thinks I am.

You have an organized look to you.
Perhaps that's not the best word. I want every minute to be three minutes. I'm really impatient. I think that's my biggest weakness. I'm just terribly impatient. I want everything to happen faster and on time.

And the process of making films is really the opposite, isn't it? It's very slow and it takes awhile to find the magic.
That's right. We were at the studio yesterday, shooting the show about day care. I had designed this scene where we needed 10 babies between the ages of eight and 15 months. So we had all these crying babies around. We were an hour and a half late.

If you don't have an ulcer this is guaranteed to give you one. I went absolutely crazy. I can't stand it when I'm kept waiting, and I can't stand to keep people waiting. So I'm really impatient about those kinds of things.

What are your strengths as a filmmaker?
I'm good at raising money—that takes time and a lot of creativity. Also, I'm a people person and that helps a lot. I like interviewing people. Actually I'd love to interview you. Turn the tables here.

What kind of people actually do appeal to you?
A person with nooks and crannies. Flat people don't interest me. There are a lot of flat people.

What do you need as an artist?
What do artists need?

No, what do *you* need?
Chaos. Most of my creative time happens in noise. I can write better at an airport. And I can think more clearly in my car and in a traffic jam than almost anywhere.

Why?
Maybe I need chaos to be creative. Quiet doesn't do it for me.

So you don't like sitting alone when you're about to write or create?
No, it doesn't work. I'm better at my computer in the office when there is craziness going around.

Because it stimulates you?
I don't know. I don't know what that's about. Maybe I've just lived in chaos too long. So I need it. I must say my best times are at a gas station before I pump my own gas.

So you write best when ...
It's always at a time when writing isn't the best idea. So I'll put a pad next to me on the car seat and work on an idea. Off-the-wall stuff. I need it as an artist.

What's a typical workday like?

None are typical. Some days I'm out, running to screenings and labs. Other days I'm mostly at my desk, responding to mail, doing the books, writing proposals, or writing scripts.

What's your preference?

Directing and producing, although I don't like all the nitty-gritty of producing. I like assembling a team. I like picking subjects, whether they're commercial or not.

What do you like about directing?

Deciding how everything should look, figuring out what environment the person we're interviewing should be in, and then how to shoot the interview—what the right angle would be. I like thinking about things like that, which has to do with directing docs. But that's quite different from directing drama.

Because you're not working with actors and a script?

Right. When you're working on a doc you're dealing mostly with real people and trying to get a good interview.

What do you do to get a good interview?

I try to engage the person I'm talking to.

By asking them certain kinds of questions?

No, it's not just asking questions. I don't usually sit with notes. I don't have a list of questions like you do.

I often have a list and then I ignore it.

Me too. I write the questions down. But I'll think more about what I want someone to say, what I need them to say for the film. Then I sort of kibbitz my way. I try to hook the person into talking about something that may have nothing to do with the interview. I try to relax them.

Are you confident about yourself in terms of your work?

Let me put it this way. I often stay up late at night or wake up in the middle of the night in cold sweats. I wonder if they're ever going to find out that I'm not who they think I am, or who I think I am.

Have you always felt this way?
Always.

Do you feel more insecure under certain situations?
Going into new things often makes me feel less secure. Up until a few years ago I really didn't have clients as such. I received grants and I was my own client. I had nobody to please but me. Once you have clients that kicks up all the self-doubts. You're no longer pleasing yourself. You're pleasing someone else. So you better be happy with what you're doing.

What do you tell yourself when you wake up in the middle of the night?
I try to tell myself that I'm good. That I'm better than most, that I work harder than most, that I'm not a mediocre kind of filmmaker.

Does that work?
Not always. I have a client now who's driving me up the wall. Everyone who's worked for her has quit and I'm about to do the same. I'm already halfway into the project. I never had that relationship with anybody. I don't like her. It makes me question myself and my ability to charm.

Is that what the middle-of-the-night voice says to you—that you're not a charmer?
Sometimes it goes beyond that and says that maybe I ought to get out of this business.

Because you feel you're not good enough?
I've never thought I wasn't good. But I've really always felt that I've been in the right place at the right time. I mean a lot of it is timing. I have lots of doubt, thoughts, from time to time.

Are those doubts exacerbated because you're a woman?
My being a woman has had pluses and minuses. For the most part I think it's worked for me because it's made me stand out. I've been unique because I'm a female and also because I'm older than most people in my industry.

Now that you've produced and directed more than 50 films

and videos what's your next plan?

I keep saying I want to do a feature and then I think, "Do you really? Are you just answering a question from all the people, who say, 'When are you going to do a feature?'"

When are you going to do a feature?

I know it's time to get on with it. But I have big doubts about it—my capacity to handle things as a producer. It's hard work. I mean it's fucking hard work. Docs are hard but features are even harder. And the kind of features I want to do . . .

What are they?

Small, personal, like *Stand By Me* and *The Trip to Bountiful*. But can I handle all the stress? I don't know—the jury's out.

Just in closing, can you think of any more "Aha!" moments in your career?

Yes, when the Fox Theatre was refurbished in Detroit. It was a 60-year anniversary and Little Caesars came to us to produce a film about this theater.

Was there something unusual about the theater?

Absolutely. It's the largest movie house in the world and the one that's survived the longest. So when they asked me to do the film I said, "Oh yeah, we'll get all those people from the old days." We actually found one of the women who was in the first chorus line in 1928. And then we found a violinist who had been playing in the pit. And when we brought them together to perform on stage some 50 years later, it was one of the most wonderful moments—it was "Aha, oh yeah, a piece of cake."

Like magic.

Right. And then you think there's no other way. You get so sure of yourself.

That's probably why you like magic.

Probably. There's no doubt. It's one of those times when you just know that's the way.

Frank Pierson: "I've spent a lifetime looking for partners. I would have loved to have found my Billy Wilder to be an I.A.L. Diamond to."

> **6** With *Cool Hand Luke*, Stuart Rosenberg still thinks that character is Jesus Christ and I think he's Camus. But Stuart filled the movie with all these Christian images . . . The cross figure keeps coming up throughout the picture. And it's absolute bull–shit. It had nothing to do with my intentions. **9**

FRANK PIERSON
Screenwriter

Fresh out of a hospital and still in pain after knee surgery, Frank Pierson nonetheless was full of energy and eager to talk about two favorite topics—creativity and screenplay writing. His own scripts include some bona fide classics: *Cat Ballou*, which he was hired to rewrite and which earned an Oscar nomination for best adaptation; *Cool Hand Luke*, also nominated for an Oscar, and *Dog Day Afternoon*, which won the Oscar in 1975. Pierson also co-wrote the script for 1990's highly acclaimed *Presumed Innocent*.

Pierson's noteworthy credits as a director include *King of the Gypsies*; the 1975 version of *A Star Is Born* starring Barbra Streisand and Kris Kristofferson, the third largest grossing musical ever filmed, and an NBC movie, *The Neon Ceiling*, which won Emmies for the performances of Lee Grant and Gig Young.

Sitting on his patio, with a breathtaking view of the Pacific Palisades, Pierson recalled how—although scripting was clearly in his blood—he did not start writing for TV until he was 33. His mother's autobiography, *Roughly Speaking*, was a '40s best-seller. She adapted it as a screenplay for Warner Brothers, then became a contract writer for Warner and RKO.

Pierson, meanwhile, saw combat during three years with the Army in the Pacific. He came home, earned a Harvard degree in cultural anthropology and, in 1951, went to work for *Time* and *Life* as a writer and field correspondent.

In 1958 he turned to TV, just as the Golden Age was waning. One moment he would write for a show such as *Playhouse 90*; the next moment the show would be canceled. For several years he produced, wrote and directed episodes of such shows as *Route 66*, *Naked City* and *Dr. Kildare*. His colleagues included John Cassavetes, Robert Altman, Bob Rafelson, Burt Schneider, Paul Mazursky, Howard Fast, Sidney Sheldon and Carl Reiner. "We were all fired more or less the same day," Pierson said.

So he went across the street to Columbia Pictures, signed on for *Cat Ballou*, and the rest is history.

Do you find that each time you write a screenplay it gets easier—or that you're facing a blank page every time?
Every time you make a movie you have to find the style for it, and then you have to find out how to do it. It's like everyone is starting all over again and you accumulate a certain amount of knowledge about the things that you're good at and the things that you'd probably best not try. But when you sit down it's a blank slate every single time. The act of finishing the movie is the act of finding out how to make it. And then you really wish you could throw it all away and start all over again. But Woody Allen is the only one who has the luxury of doing that.

Can you talk about writing *Presumed Innocent*?
I learned about the artificiality of mystery writing, which I'd never done before. You have all the information, and it is more an issue of which information you choose to share with the audience and with your characters and how much the various characters know about each other as you go along. That is a very artificial way for me to work. I prefer to work on a more unconscious level in terms of writing the scenes and even constructing the story, even though I do work from an outline, unlike a lot of other screenwriters. So I found it a peculiarly unsatisfying experience. I don't think I'll do another one like it.

What was your relationship like with the director?
Alan [Pakula] and I had a lot of differences about the story, which is one reason I insisted he also put his name on the screenplay. He did some things I did not agree with. I wanted to cut 30 pages and leap into the story much later. I just felt that the audi-

ence was going to guess it was the wife who did it, and I was much more interested in another aspect of the story.

Which was what?

Scott Turow, the novelist, lied to his readers the first day of the trial. The main character, Rusty, sees evidence that shakes him up. It occurs to him that his lifelong faith in the system may have been misplaced, that he may be ground up and thrown away. It's utterly devastating, because his whole philosophy of life has been denied validity. So that night, he goes home and his wife says, "Come on up. Let me rub your back." And he says, "No, no, I have to stay up." For the first time in years he lights up a cigarette. It's one of the best chapters in the novel.

When does this take place?.

It's about page 200 of a 500-page-novel. He's thinking about his life, about how he always believed in the system and about how he failed his wife. It's revealed in the chapter that he told his wife about his affair, how they battled it out and it was all put behind them. He realizes in the end that there's nothing he can do about the situation, except simply stick with it, and that if he is considered innocent all he can do is try and live his life in a better way. It's a terribly moving piece, because you know he had to think this through for himself. It's a devastating turning point in his life, where he's losing all his life's beliefs.

And that's the story you were interested in telling?

Yes, but a couple hundred pages later in the novel, you discover that that's not the reason he sat up all night. He sat up all night because he saw evidence in the courtroom that day that told him, unequivocally, that his wife was the one who did it. Well, that is such a lie to the reader, the kind of thing that I don't believe you can do to an audience. But the director said that the book worked the way it did for an enormous number of people and we shouldn't fool around with that. So he didn't want to make this change.

How would you have changed the script?

I was going to do that first day in court where he comes home and, just as in the book, his wife tells him to come upstairs but he says he wants to be by himself. Then goes right to the toolbox in the cellar because suddenly he realizes that they have a tool in the house which makes wounds that are difficult to identify. I actually found [an example of] this tool. Anyway, there's blood and hair on it, and we realize that he realizes that his wife has done it. He walks upstairs, puts the tool down by the kitchen sink and mixes himself a drink. He hears a noise, turns around and his wife says, "What are you going to do?" And it all comes out between them.

That scene was in the movie.

Yes, but at the end. I wanted to move that scene up where she says, "I'll testify for you, I never meant for it to go this far. I don't know how I could have been this insane." She would give essentially the same speech that she gives at the end. And he says, "It wouldn't do any good, nobody'd believe you. They'd think you were trying to save me. It's too late, all we can do is get through this to the end."

The rest of the movie would become a drama that has to do with two people knowing that at the end of it there has to be some resolution. Will he let his child know that his wife is a murderer? Can he leave his child with this woman? How is she going to appease the guilt that she feels, while at the same time having to preserve an absolutely perfect front in the courtroom? But Pakula felt that that was a completely different story. And it is, indeed.

It's a more character-driven story.

You're dead right. In fact, we rehearsed scenes with Harrison Ford that way and everything worked. But Pakula wanted to do the book, so we did.

Do you regret having done it that way?

I was working as a screenwriter for Alan, which means you're a hired hand. I wouldn't second-guess that, no. If I were going to direct it by myself? I don't know whether that would have worked any better than what he did. And the movie was a success.

The audience could have known more about the characters, especially the wife.

Well, part of the problem was, as I said, that he shot an enormously long screenplay—about 150 pages. And a screenplay should only be about 115 pages. I see certain things just flashing by because he had to cut too much, like some of the beginnings and endings of scenes. It's amazing to me that the audience understands it as well as they do. So I guess we did a pretty damn good job, because it still works. Nonetheless, I'm so aware of what's missing that I can't judge it for myself at all. But I do love the way Bonnie (Bedelia) read that speech at the end.

What movies did you write that were satisfying?
Dog Day Afternoon. It was brilliantly directed and acted. And there was the issue of craft. Well, let me back up and speak generally. Knowing how to make the movie is an issue of solving problems. You have one problem after another and the first one is how you begin. What you're saying to an audience is, "This is the way we're going to spend the next two hours of our lives together."

Does the audience need to know right away what kind of film they are watching?
Definitely. They need to know very quickly what it is that's going to be happening with them, and also to feel secure that you're not going to bludgeon them or bore them. But there was another problem with the beginning. We had a situation in which three people are setting out to rob a bank. Guns are out and it ain't funny. There's a machine gun in a case, and when you look at John Cazale you are seeing a homicidal character who is dangerous because of his infantile attitude toward life. And so the problem was, how do you let an audience know that it's all right for them to laugh?

How did you let them know?
By carefully crafting the initial sequence. Three guys go in, the guns are out, there's danger and they're waiting for the proper moment. When the last person is let out of the bank and the tension is building, this other kid sidles up to Sonny and says, "I got bad vibes here." A little ripple goes through the audience. Then he says, "Whaddya talkin' about for Christ's sake, the banks are gonna be closed," which was an odd line in that context.

So you have moments when the audience can laugh.

Right. And then you keep going. You build tension, and then he finally pulls out the automatic gun, points it at the teller and says, "I'm gonna blow your fuckin' guts all over the walls." This was the moment when we knew that the whole thing was going to turn in everyone's face, and from there on anything could happen.

Are there visual or technical things you can do that give the audience permission to laugh?

Yes. When you do comedy, you light everything from edge to edge so everybody can see everything, so there are no surprises. The technical aspect has become so damned important in film. You look at a movie like *Prizzi's Honor*—which was a success and it's a lovely picture; but in the theater I went to, the audience was constantly sitting forward in their seats and saying, "What? Did she say that?" Because the dialogue has a slight little spin to it. Nothing is quite the way you expect it to be.

But it was meant to be a comedy?

Yes. And of course John Huston knew that, but Jack Nicholson claims that he never realized that it was a comedy.

But you're saying the sound track interfered with the comedy?

Yes. The problem for me was that the balance between the various tracks was out of sync. The dialogue was down and there was an odd spin to it, so they were not meaning exactly what they were saying. Consequently the audience was straining to hear the whole time, and you could see from their body language that they experienced the movie as a drama. You watch a comedy from down here and a drama from up here. But Huston was a darkly ironic character, so he sometimes tripped over the comedy. *Beat the Devil*, which has now become a cult classic film, was an absolute disaster when it first came out because nobody got the idea at the beginning that it was supposed to be funny.

How did you come up with the idea for *Dog Day Afternoon*?

I got it out of an FBI report of a real robbery somewhere in Virginia. The robber came in and put the gun in the head teller's face and said, "Give me all your money." And you know those little triangular signs that say, "Next Window Please"? The teller put one of them up! So I stuck that in the screenplay. That was going to be the joke on which we would build everything, and then everything would unravel. The whole point being that in the middle of the worst things that happen in our lives, life goes on, people need to go to the bathroom! And how do you cope with those things? Intrinsically it's funny, which constantly releases the tension as we get to the end where we know something dreadful is going to happen. But I hope we don't know exactly what it is.

So once you found the beginning did things become easier?
Not really. Because when we started rehearsing, and the teller pushes out the sign, the director, Sidney Lumet, asked who told her to do that. She said that it was in the stage directions. And he said he didn't see that. And then I said, "But that's the beginning of the joke." And he responded, "But that would be funny." And then I knew we were in trouble. I suddenly realized that he was not thinking about this sequence in the same way I was.

Which had to do with giving the audience permission to laugh?
Exactly. I'd been working on it for months. But it was a screenplay that Sidney didn't receive until it was complete. If we had been working on it together as we had in the past, we might have agreed more. So we went ahead with the sign. But when we got to the dress rehearsal and Al [Pacino] had the rifle in a box which was for long-stemmed roses, he couldn't get it out of the box without the damn thing getting tangled up in the ribbon. Of course that was funny, and that went right into the script. Then the problem was to convince everybody to take the sign out, because you couldn't have both. There's a certain order in which things happen.

Did you ever meet the person whose character Pacino was based upon?
No. He was in a contract dispute with Warner Brothers over his share of the net profit, so every time I visited the prison, he refused to see me. I just had to proceed on my own by interviewing his family and everybody who'd ever known him, including the people in the bank. But that became so confusing because it

was like they were talking about a different character. Some said he was kind and loving, some said he was brutal, and some said he was funny.

But he was all of that in the movie.
The thing that was difficult was finding some common element or spine to that character so it would all make sense. I got to the point where I almost quit because I couldn't figure him out. There wasn't anything but the newspaper reports, which described what he did and said. But if an actor asked why he was behaving a certain way, I had no answer. So I went through all the research material one last time and I began to realize that there was one common element to everyone's comments.

Which was?
Everybody felt he had betrayed them. So I looked up the meaning of the word betray—it means you have made a promise or a contract to someone and have failed to deliver on it. Then I realized that the people who felt most betrayed by him were the people to whom he was the closest. And finally the character who began to emerge for me was like a wizard.

In what sense?
He imagines that he has the power to fulfill your dreams and hopes. He can make you whole and then you will be able to give him back the love that he desperately needs and which he expressed to you. Of course this is impossible under the best of circumstances, and especially for this neurotic, working-class guy from Brooklyn.

How did this specifically translate into action?
He would never let his wife, who was grotesquely fat, diet. Because it would be like an admission that she was fat. So he'd say, "Honey, you're not fat. You're just the way I like 'em." After a while it led to a kind of infantilization of her. And this kind of behavior made sense in terms of the bank robbery itself.

How so?
Because Sonny marries this homosexual who imagines that he needs to have his woman's body freed from his male body by a sex change operation. So Sonny robs the bank to get the money

for this operation so his lover will be happy. And the lover's reaction is, "Jesus Christ, I didn't ask you to rob a fucking bank! Are you outa your mind?" So now you have a dramatic character that you know how to write. He's the kind of character who says, "Are you comfortable? Is there anything I can get for you?"

And do the other characters respond to that?

The needy ones do, which leads to a bonding that is built around a tacit understanding that you're going to do this for me. And when he's unable to deliver, they begin to back away or complain; and he says, "I did everything for you and I get back shit." And they respond with, "I never asked you for anything," which would erupt into a fistfight or whatever. And everything in his life went that way, with him feeling bruised. Now you have a character you can move through this situation in the bank, and any situation. You know what he's going to do.

So that's the common thread that you were talking about.

Yeah, exactly. And that makes it possible to write the individual scenes, and it also leads to the next step, which has to do with constructing the story. Because I want the eventual retribution to come about because of the very thing that makes Sonny what he is. In other words, it's not just the mere fact that he stayed in the bank too long and someone tripped the silent alarm that got him into trouble. He stayed in the bank because of the kind of person he was. He could have gotten out with what little money there was.

You mentioned the idea of constructing a story.

There are two major turning points in a film. You trap some people in a situation, and there's a period where everybody could get back to square one if they just didn't go on being who they are. But at some point, somebody does something and they can never get back to where they were before, but they don't know where the future lies. Then you have the period of uncertainty where essentially the characters are exploring alternatives of extricating themselves from the situation, of resolving it in a new way, of bringing about a new synergistic resolution to things, and again their inner problems and mutual antagonisms get in the way. Then you get to the second turning point which can occur anywhere in here, and sometimes very close to the end. It's where they suddenly realize, "Oh, this is how it's gonna go," and now we're going to go from there to the end.

Is that part of the technique you use as a writer?

Yes. Of course, you take a play like *Waiting for Godot* and you realize that it does not have any of those things, so all general-izations are false. But as a working method, this is more or less how I go about it. I was looking for a way in which that moment when they're trapped in the bank seals their fate. And it's brought about by the very thing that brought Sonny there in the first place—his insistence, his desperate need to be of help—to worry about things like, "Should I let them go to the toilet?"

How much rehearsal did you have for this film?

We had the luxury of three weeks of rehearsal because we were able to hire the cast for the run of the show since every-body was virtually in every scene and we essentially had just one location. But about four days into it I'm sitting with Al Pacino in his living room and everyone has these long faces and the producer is saying, "Look, what Al's talking about is really just a dialogue polish." At which point Al gets down on all fours and runs around the room barking like a dog. And I said, "You know, I don't think Al is talking about a dialogue polish."

What was he talking about?

It turned out that he did not want to play a homosexual and I asked specifically what he objected to. There's a scene where Sonny and his lover have to say goodbye. In the film, the scene plays over the telephone. But I originally had written it to play in the street with Al standing just inside the front door and Chris Sarandon standing just outside the bank with the police officer holding him by the belt so he couldn't be pulled into the bank and added to the hostages. There are 2,000 police officers, and behind them the entire neighborhood screaming, "Faggot!" And so these two people have to play the one scene in their life that most cries out for privacy in this maelstrom of derision. And they succeed in getting through it and ignoring it. At the end they kiss each other on the lips. Then the crowd goes really crazy and snaps us back to reality.

How did Pacino respond to the kiss?

He said, "I'm not gonna do it. I'm not gonna play any scene where I have to be in the presence of the guy." I actually invented a way that we could show their wedding, and he said, "You can't show them together at all. All the stuff about the sexuality of their relationship and the joke is out." So I said to the producer, "Let's do what we did when Al quit the first time—send it to Dustin [Hoffman]."

I didn't realize that Pacino had quit once before.
Yeah. He had just come from *The Godfather* and was exhausted. I guess this thing was bubbling in him at that time, but he hadn't identified if for himself yet. He said he thought it was a terrific screenplay but he couldn't do it because he was too depressed.

But you talked him into it?
Actually, we sent the script to Dustin. And when Al heard that, he asked for it back. He said, "Look, before you do that I'd just like to say something to you. You've had relationships, I know you've been married a couple of times. And when you're playing the really big scenes in those relationships, especially when things are falling apart and all you can do is get out of it the best way you can, how often does sex come into it?" I said, "Never." And he said, "Look, you cannot take away from the audience's mind the fact that a man married a man. But why can't you just write a story about two people who love each other and can't find any way to get what they want?"

How did you respond?
I said, "You sonofabitch; why didn't you say that six months ago when I had time to deal with it?" Al said, "I really wish you would do it—if you agree." And I said, "Absolutely. You're dead right." It turned out rather easy to do. What I was left with were two scenes between the two of them on the telephone—one in which Sarandon kisses him off entirely, and then the Sarandon character calls him back.
In the course of that conversation we discover that ultimately the reason Sarandon calls him back is because the police have threatened him with being an accessory after the fact. He's trying to get Pacino to say that he was not part of it, and of course Pacino is betrayed again. So what you see in the arc of those two

long phone calls is a little mini-film which parallels the arc of their real-life relationship. But those phone calls defy all cinematic rules.

How so?

You're not supposed to break scenes up like that. But not being able to show them together was a brilliant inspiration on Al's part. It saved the movie. It would have been funnier, but it's funny enough. And it ran the danger of appearing to be homophobic.

Is *Dog Day Afternoon* your most satisfying film?

Yes, because it's the closest to what I wrote and I did my best work. One of the difficulties in my career as a director is that I've given myself some rather bad scripts.

Such as?

I'd rather not say.

You did write and direct *A Star Is Born*.

I co-wrote it. The screenplay was originated by Joan Didion and John Dunne. They claim they never saw any of the original versions, but I have to politely say that I just don't believe them. What they did was a rather harder-edged and documentary approach to the same story set in the rock music world. Well, the minute Barbra came on board it changed right back into the romantic melodrama that it's always been, and what always made it work. What I did was take off the hard edges and go back to the 1936 version. Dorothy Parker, among other people, worked on that version.

Can you talk about the directing end of things?

Some director once said that writing was either the first half of the directing process or directing was the last half of the writing process. That's perfectly true. I've spent a lifetime looking for partners. I would have loved to have found my Billy Wilder to be an I.A.L. Diamond to. But I was never able to, so consequently you go through life kind of hit or miss, and it's amazing how close you can be and yet how far apart.

I mean, with *Cool Hand Luke*, Stuart Rosenberg still thinks that character is Jesus Christ and I think he's Camus. But Stuart filled the movie with all these Christian images. After Paul Newman's eaten the 50 eggs and he's passed out, we see him sprawled out as a figure on the cross. The cross figure keeps coming up throughout the picture. And it's absolute bullshit. It had nothing to do with my intentions.

Do you feel the film worked?
Yeah, I think it's a good film. And it still holds up. But there are scenes that I look at and say, "Oh, Jesus, if that's what you wanted to do I could have written you a scene that would have worked so much better."

Can you talk more about the unconscious process?
When you approach a tough scene and you don't know what the solutions are going to be and you discard all the ways it's been done before—the easy ways, the melodramatic ways and the tricky ways—you say, "How am I going to solve this? Where is the idea going to come from?" At that point the only place it's going to come from is the unconscious.

You've made a connection, I assume, before you've committed yourself. There's something in the material that lures you and you don't know what it is. It's the writing of it, and the making of it, that helps you find out what it is. What is this connection I feel here? That answer is going to emerge in a dream, or in a nightmare, or when you're driving on the freeway, or when you're just sort of doing exercises.

Where do you write?
At home. And I have an office as well.

Are there particular hours that you like to write?
From 10 to 12. Then I have lunch and spend the afternoon going over what I wrote that morning. And I might be back at the computer at 11 or 12 o'clock at night. So it's never away from your thoughts.

Do you write every day?
Yes, even on people's birthdays and holidays. Laptops are a godsend because the most important thing about writing is to addict yourself to it. So that you cannot not write, in the same way that a heroin addict cannot *not* prowl the streets to find the

goddamned heroin. And that will make you constantly focused on it. Every day, you're going to have to put something down, because otherwise you're going to kick your dog, you're going to be rude to strangers, and you're going to estrange your wife.

And you find that two hours every day works for you?
Yes. I devote myself to putting down the thoughts that have been occurring to me the rest of the time. Or if nothing else occurs, I ask myself the most elementary questions—like what is the conflict between the two characters? Or what would this person do if they were confronted with such and such? It's amazing how often something will emerge that winds up in some form in the screenplay. But as a writer you don't know where this is going to come from. All you can do is simply open yourself up in any way that you find to do it.

Such as?
By getting drunk, by taking dope, by simply staring out the window, or reaching over and gently stroking your Oscar, like a talisman. Because the unconscious from which this idea is going to emerge is the very place that we defend against. But we have to take the plunge, going there amongst our demons. All of a sudden something emerges and you say, "My God, nobody's going to understand that."

Can you think of a specific time when that happened?
Yes. The very much quoted line from *Cool Hand Luke*, "What we have here is a failure to communicate." That came out of my looking out over the Pacific Ocean and trying to think of what I wanted him to say. All of a sudden that line came. And I looked at it and I said, "Oh shit, that's good." But then my next thought was, "This redneck can't say that." So I spent the rest of the day writing a little explanation that I put into the stage directions which said that in the Florida prison system, in order to gain advancement, the bureaucratic process required prison officers to take a certain number of courses in criminology and penology at the state university. So we understood where he would hear words like that.

Did anyone ever question the line?
No, to my astonishment, they didn't. But the point is that

instinct came out of somewhere, and my first impulse was to expunge it. Then I justified it and then I realized it didn't need to be justified. But that's what I mean about the unconscious aspects of the writing process that make it very difficult. We are probing into those areas which we defend against.

The director, at least from my experience, has difficulty in a different way. That comes when you're on the floor and you've got a sequence that's not working. You don't have the time and you can't figure out how to make it work. That's when it's really hard because you can't make the actors play something when you realize that the damned thing isn't right. So you improvise.

Can you think of an example of when that happened to you as a director?
The Looking Glass War was a movie that we prepared over a long period of time. It was based on a John Le Carre novel. To get the picture made, the producer and I had to cut this and change that. We had four days of reading rehearsals before we went off to Spain to start shooting. But it wasn't working, so finally we cabled the studio and said, "Look, it's not gonna work and the best advice is to cut our losses and stop production."

Were you able to stop it?
No, because by that time the people who ran the studio had gone off to the West Indies to a retreat. So we got back a cable saying, "Best first week ever seen. Continue the good work. Congratulations from Columbia Studios." We had to somehow hold ourselves together for four months while we finished the picture. Making a film under those conditions is really shattering.

Nicholas Kazan talks of writers as "receptacles" and how you have to get yourself to that pure state. How do you do that?
That's what I mean about you get drunk, you take drugs, you massage your Oscar if you have one, or you meditate. These are reasons writers are terrible people to live with. If you have small children in the house you should not write in the house with them.

Did your writing affect your family life?

No question about it. But I'd prefer not to talk about it. All I can say is I've spent a lot of years in deep analysis to deal with this. And, you know, if I were in the state of mind that I think I'm in now when I was 20 or 25, I certainly would have dealt with it in a more constructive way and protected my family from the demons that were aroused in me and drove me crazy. During the first part of your career, as Nick puts it in a sort of nice way, the writer is a receptacle—but that's almost a reverence that he's paying to the pain and terror he endures in that state.

Can you talk more about your analysis?

I went into analysis because there was somebody in me that was trying to kill me, and I had to find out. Otherwise, I knew that I was not going to live. So I went in a state of emotional crisis. But once I got past that, because of the particular person that I went into analysis with, I began to realize that there was something far more to it, that it could be a kind of voyage to the spirit, an exploratory voyage that at first I was very scared of. I was afraid that by investigating the process I would destroy my ability to write. A friend of mine once said, "What are you going to do when you're not angry anymore?"

But you were able to work that out.

Yes, but it took me a while. And I was already 45 when I started therapy. I asked the analyst why he started working with me at such an advanced age. And he said something that was very pleasing to me. He said, "Because I sense in you still a flexibility and an ability to change."

Did that help with your work as a writer?

It helped me with my whole life. But I diverged from something I started to say. And that is, in the early phases of one's career, when you're confronting these things, you don't know whether you can write a scene that actors can play. You confront that moment when nothing is coming and you're thinking, "Jesus, I've taken their money, maybe I'm going to have to send it back. Or I'll just call my agent and get myself out of this."

And that's what you went through when Pacino wanted you to rework your script?

Yes. I was ready to call my agents before I went back and took one last look at that mass of material so I could understand who that character was. Early in your career you reach for the easy things—the sitcoms, the Westerns, the genre stories—which provide you with ready-made elements. If you're going to probe in these areas, it can drive you nuts. Sometimes you have the feeling that no one understands you and you wind up driving your Porsche in the mountains all night long.

What does delving into "these areas" mean to you?

I still don't like to think about it consciously; but I've discovered there's a certain kind of character to whom I'm attracted. That's the lonely outsider. I look at the people I've written best, and they're all outsiders. Rusty, in *Presumed Innocent*, is a guy who—despite the fact that he has built all the accoutrements of family and social amenities and life philosophy, which is intertwined with the way in which he lives—is absolutely alone.

Do you feel that essentially most writers write the same story over and over?

Yes. The question is, when do you become tired of it? If the story is good enough, it has enough variations.

What did you learn from therapy that helped you with your writing?

Oh, a complete revision of the psychodynamics of my family life as a kid.

Which was?

My father was a very glamorous character, a very handsome guy who was called "Pop," which is a demeaning name for a father. He couldn't keep a job and he was always doing crazy things. In 1930, when he couldn't find a job, he played a Santa Claus who jumped out of a plane with a parachute, bringing symbolic presents to the children of Stratford, Connecticut. He was the one who always wrecked the family and my mother was the strong woman who suffered but hid it all underneath this terrifying, brilliant exterior. She wound up writing her autobiography, which was made into a movie with Rosalind Russell playing her and Jack Carson playing my father. So she became a screenwriter and had a career for about eight years at Warner Brothers.

But you said your understanding of the family changed.

I realized that the dynamics were not really that way at all—
my father completely hid himself in order to allow her to play
that role. And to the extent that the family had any stability at
all, he was the strong one and she was the one who was
absolutely out of control. That's simplified, but there was a
major re-evaluation of my perception.

**Was there a turning point in your work as a result of your
therapy?**

I don't think so. I just worked faster and better. And fortunately I can do those things that interest me—to the extent that the
business allows anybody to do that.

Do you think the business has changed a great deal?

I think it highly unlikely that we could get *Dog Day Afternoon*
done now. In fact, (screenwriter) Bob Towne was saying the
other day that he could get *Shampoo* made but he didn't think he
could make *Chinatown* now.

Another difference is each studio used to have an identifiable
style. There was an MGM musical as opposed to a Columbia
musical, or a Warner Brothers film noir as opposed to a
Columbia film noir. But now the studios are all broken up and
each movie is a unique thing. Some are the inspiration of the
writer, some are a producer's idea, and the director tries to bring
it into fruition.

We're just emerging right now from a period in which Disney
has been trying to reinstate the old corporate authorship style.
But it doesn't work very well for them, because if you want to
make a movie which you control you are less likely to hire someone with an enormous run of successes behind him, who will tell
you how to do your movie. You'll hire someone right out of film
school whom you can tell what to do. And then when he fucks
up, you'll hire another one.

**Also, isn't there quite a difference in salaries between the
established and new writer?**

You can hire 10 writers for $150,000 apiece instead of one
writer for a million-five. And by the end of that period there are
so many drafts that no one knows who did what to whom or
why. Anyway, that's sort of the general background situation

against which we all work. But when you come right down to making a film, you eventually get led into the same psychological area from which all creativity derives.

Which is?
Seeing things that you've looked at before in new combinations and in new ways that elicit a very strong emotional reaction. A lot of psychologists and philosophers around the turn of the century were examining the issue of creativity, particularly in the area of comedy.

Why comedy?
Because it's easiest to deconstruct the process. Comedy is a very intellectual exercise. Laughs are very carefully crafted and planned. They just don't happen spontaneously. That goes back to the famous old joke—dying is easy, comedy is hard.

It's sort of like the difference between surgery and internal medicine. In surgery you lay back the skin and you see the muscles and it's a procedure which is out in the open. Whereas in internal medicine you're looking at vague signs and the temperature is going up a little bit, but you don't really know why. Because the construction of comedy is a more craftsman-like procedure, it makes it more accessible in terms of trying to analyze it and deconstruct it to see how it works, so that we know what it is that makes us laugh.

What do you think your strengths and weaknesses are as a writer?
I like to work with character. Like most men, I don't write women as well as I would like to, but I think I write them better than a lot of men do. One of the difficulties in answering this question is that some of the best screenplays I've written have not been made.

Such as?
In 1980 I got a commission from Warner Brothers to do a story about three out-of-work steelworkers in Pittsburgh and what happens to them. They are the middle generation—too old to be retrained and too young to have sufficient stake in the pension fund. So they've got to find a strength inside themselves. Each one of them crumbles and then finds an anger which is going to

lead him to revenge himself. The main couple have their love for each other, and they'll find a way. I loved that screenplay and was crying with love and affection at the end. But these were the Reagan years, and the studio found the story terribly depressing and wouldn't make it. If I had gotten it done three months earlier I think we might have gone into production.

When you look back over your career do you have any major regrets?

Woody Allen once said, when somebody asked him a similar question, "If I had to live my life over again, on the whole I'd do everything the same except maybe I wouldn't go see *The Magus*." Regrets? Yeah, enormous regrets. Existential regrets in the sense that going through life is a matter of doors either remaining closed or slamming closed on you. You have so many choices when you're born, depending on what class you're in. I was very fortunate for a lot of reasons, and there were a million doors opened. But suddenly you realize that door's closed, and I'm never going to be able to do that again. And so there are a few along the way that I wish that I had opened at that time.

Do you know which ones?

No. I'm saying it's an existential feeling of loss which may only mean that my appetite is too big.

Do you think that different people have varying degrees of creativity or need to express that creativity?

I think some people have one creative moment in their life and then there are people like Robin Williams, where everything is exploding at every moment. But in either case, creativity has to do with seeing associations between two feelings or a feeling and an idea, which have never been seen or thought of before in this new context—which then gives rise to an evolutionary new idea.

That is only a crude way of expressing Henri Bergson's theory of creative evolution. The creative process is very destructive because those new levels of understanding destroy everything in the arena. Our level of understanding before that is gone. After Newton made the connection between apples falling off trees and the rotation of the planets around the sun and realized they were all related in one grand scheme, nobody could ever think about the universe in the same way again.

The
Trip to Bountiful
Interviews

Carlin Glynn and Pete Masterson: "I think the basic thing is that Pete and I are trained in the same way. So there's a basic respect for the way we each work and there's a lot of shorthand sometimes. Of course, there are also arguments."

6 You have to find the justification for what she does. Nobody gets up in the morning and says, 'I'm going to be a sonofabitch today.' 9

CARLIN GLYNN
Actress

6 I used to give long lectures about the backgrounds of the characters and the situation, and now everybody is part of the discussion. The more I expose the actors and the designers and everybody else to the material and the more we discuss it, the more they come to it on their own terms and they feel like they thought of it—and maybe they did. 9

PETE MASTERSON
Director

Carlin Glynn and Pete Masterson share a home, three children, a creative sensibility, and a great deal of success in several plays and movies. In 1979 Masterson, who developed *The Best Little Whorehouse in Texas* with Glynn at the Actors Studio, won a Drama Desk Award as best director and was nominated for a Tony Award for direction and as author of the book. Glynn, who created the role of the bordello madam, won a Tony. When the play went to London, Glynn won the Lawrence Olivier Award as best actress in a musical.

Masterson and Glynn were young apprentices when they met at the Alley Theatre in Houston. Both started out as actors. Besides winning a Tony for *Whorehouse*, Glynn won the Joseph Jefferson Award for *Pal Joey* at the Goodman Theatre in Chicago. She has worked in such films as *Three Days of the Condor, Sixteen Candles, Gardens of Stone* and *Convicts*. On TV she has co-hosted WABC's *Good Morning New York* and co-starred with George C. Scott in *Mr. President* on the Fox Network.

Masterson also has enjoyed success as an actor. He starred in *The Trial of Lee Harvey Oswald* on Broadway in 1967 and landed major roles in *The Great White Hope* and *That Championship Season*. His film acting includes roles in *The Exorcist* and *The Stepford Wives*. But Masterson began to write, as well; and he was directing at the Actors Studio when he read an article about a whorehouse that had closed in Texas. Hence the play that he co-wrote, directed and stayed with for four years.

After the successful New York and London runs of *Whorehouse*, Masterson was ready to expand once again—this time into film directing. An opportunity presented itself in a conversation with Robert Redford at the Sundance Institute, created by Redford to develop films and plays. Redford suggested that Masterson find material that was "small and meaningful" to him.

Masterson immediately thought of *The Trip to Bountiful*, a play written by a distant cousin, Horton Foote, who asked that Glynn play Jessie Mae, one of the leading roles. And so once again Masterson and Glynn were working together.

Interviewed in their Fifth Avenue apartment overlooking Central Park, Glynn and Masterson alternated leaving the room to take business and personal calls, including one from actress daughter Mary Stuart Masterson. All were awaiting release of *Convicts*, starring James Earl Jones and Robert Duvall. Once again it was a family venture: Horton Foote writing, Carlin Glynn acting and Pete Masterson, wearing one of his favorite hats, directing.

Carlin, you once said, "I have a real affinity to the characters I play"—and that you didn't want to play Jessie Mae as a shrew in *The Trip to Bountiful*, so you tried to "back-door" that role. What does that mean?

Glynn: Well, it has to do with creating a character's agenda as opposed to what the film's agenda may be. I think I was very concerned when Horton asked Pete if I would do the role, because I could see all the traps in the character—the stereotypes, the one-dimensional aspect of her. So I worked very hard to get away from that by "back-dooring it"—which means looking at the situation from this woman's eyes. I worked on an element of sexuality with John Heard, who played her husband, Ludie. They're cramped into this small house with his mother, and all they have is a clear glass door to separate them.

And you're very attracted to each other.

Glynn: Yes, and so I thought it was important to create that aspect of their relationship. I also tried to find the little girl in myself 'cause I think in a way Jessie Mae never grew up. I felt she was having a bad 36 hours but she wasn't a bad person. I wanted it to be that she wished her mother-in-law would behave, but she didn't want her to die. I think there is a feeling in all of us, certainly actors, that we want to be approved of, so you hate to be the bad guy. And for that reason I didn't go to dailies. I always go to dailies, but I just couldn't bear to see Geraldine (Page) and John being so adorable—and I was afraid I'd pull back just to get approval.

So you had to keep concentrating on what she felt.

Glynn: Right. Here she is with her husband and mother-in-law, sitting up in the middle of the night. She barely gets out of the house—even for a Coke. She can't afford anything, her husband's been sick for a year, and she's cramped up with this woman who sings hymns all day long. So back-dooring means creating a very strong agenda. And what's been most gratifying to me is that 80 percent of the people who see this movie may not like the character, but they genuinely understand her. Especially older women who are mother-in-laws and married women with mother-in-laws.

In fact, on opening night in New York somebody came up to me and said, "Miss Glynn, I really enjoyed your work, and I'm gonna go home and work things out with my mother-in-law and my mother, before it's too late." When you hear something like that you know that you've had an effect and that the film is about something that people relate to.

Pete, what do you think was the most creative aspect of your work on the film?

Masterson: I don't know if I can answer that. It all adds up to one film, so you don't know which thing you would leave out.

Glynn: I think your having the idea to do the whole thing is the most creative thing.

At Sundance Institute?

Masterson: We didn't develop it there, but that's where the idea came to us. Redford said I should pick something that was small and meaningful to me to develop, and Carlin reminded me how much I liked the play. I'd always talked about it, and so I just called Horton right then. I'd read it, and seen a revival of it around 1960. And so I was ready to do it even though I had never directed a film before.

What was your next step?

Masterson: Horton and I worked on this script, because it was only a play at first. I thought he had already written the screen-play but he hadn't. Then I called Neil Spisak, a designer whom I liked very much, and a cinematographer named Fred Murphy. He was the only guy I talked to who didn't have an attitude that he was smarter than a first-time director. Whenever I'd say that I didn't know how to do something he'd say, "You shouldn't know how to do that, that's my job. Let's talk about it." You have to be able to say you don't know. That's the number one rule, because they'll find you out. And all I knew was that we were using 24-millimeter lenses a lot.

The scenes are almost little vignettes and plays in and of themselves.

Masterson: One of the key things I did was to plan the entire shoot with the cinematographer. We went through the film saying, "Where do we start this scene, how do we make this scene different from that scene, how do we keep the interest going visually?" So we knew exactly what to do when we got to the set. We also rehearsed for two weeks, and that was tremendously valuable. We learned a lot.

I remember the first day of rehearsal I said, "I just want to get one thing straight—this is not about a sweet little old lady and a wimpy son and a mean daughter-in-law. It's about all the relationships." Geraldine said, "Thank God!" I said, "They're human beings, and they're in a situation in which they get on each other's nerves but Geraldine is not a saint." One of the first things we did was to dispel that myth. So you can see her trying different ways to irritate Jessie Mae.

I think the key thing is that they all did seem very human.
Masterson: Yes, and each of the characters learns something. In the beginning, they're cooped up in this little place and Ludie has a horror of going back to his home where he grew up. He doesn't even want to see it. Yet, what Geraldine gives him in the end is an understanding of what you get from the land, what you take away from it. You take your strength from it for the rest of your life even though you can't go back and reclaim it. Because it's not the same. But the distributors didn't like that ending. They wanted Geraldine to stay there. And I said, "What would she do? She'd starve to death."
Glynn: Then they begged you to let her die.

Why did they want her to stay?
Masterson: Because they thought the ending we had was a sad ending. Yeah, it was a sad ending. They have to go back and try to get along in this little place, and you know they won't. But at least for today, they are going to try.

Which was uplifting.
Masterson: I don't mind that. But you don't want to let 'em off too easy.

What do you think made this movie so special?
Masterson: I think we all understood it. Whenever I direct

something I like to know what made the writer write it, because sometimes it's not evident. So I asked Horton. And he said, "Well, I heard a story when I was young about this woman who was in love with this man, but her father wouldn't let him marry her, 'cause he wasn't good enough for his daughter. But the man continued to love her the rest of his life, passed by the house and greeted her every day." The man happened to be one of my ancestors, one of my cousins.

Anyway, when we got to that moment when Geraldine says that she didn't love her husband, it didn't have quite as much impact as I thought it should. Geraldine was wonderful, but it seemed like we were missing something since the whole movie was based on that moment.

So what did you do?
Masterson: I told Geraldine that even though we had the shot we wanted to try it one more time to see if we couldn't go a little deeper personally. I said, "Do anything you want, because this is an extra." Then I told the cinematographer that I was going to start the scene with a two shot and I wanted to move into a single. But I said, "I don't want you to move the camera until the emotion works. I want the emotion to motivate the camera rather than just a word, and I don't know when that's going to happen."

So you waited for that moment to happen?
Masterson: Yes, we started with a two shot and when something started to happen I tapped Fred and he started to move in. All of a sudden it exploded. I mean, the emotion took over so much that Geraldine couldn't even talk. She got through it, and she kept looking over her shoulder to see if anybody was watching her cry. When we finally ended, she said, "Well, at least that was different."

But Fred wanted to do it again because he said it was kind of messy and Rebecca [De Mornay] was bouncing in and out of the frame. That's what the operator watches, the framing. He's not really seeing the performance. At any rate, I said, "No, we're not gonna do it again, print it."

And quite honestly, I thought that that was an Academy Award-winning moment. It was different than any other moment. But Geraldine thought it was too much. And Horton thought it was too emotional. But they were both easy to talk out of their concerns.

It's interesting how you can start out with one vision and have it change into something else.
Masterson: It always does.

How long did it take to shoot that scene?
Masterson: Well, we had a grueling day of filming. We were on a bus for 18 hours. Actually we were on a sound stage. There was a guy shaking the bus and running by with lights.

Carlin, didn't you improvise the scene where Geraldine kisses you?
Glynn: It wasn't improvised; it happened while the camera was turning.
Masterson: But you didn't plan on doing it. So in a way it was improvised.
Glynn: Yeah, we didn't plan to do it. In fact, it was a stunning moment for me, because I didn't know it was going to happen. I had a hard time sitting on the emotion.

Which was?
Glynn: To not just burst into tears. The take Pete picked, you can tell she's really moved even though she's lighting a cigarette. But it would be wrong for her to bawl in front of this woman. I mean this is war. It was a beautiful moment.

And I remember another moment after we've had the fight over the recipe. She comes into my bedroom where I'm smoking and says, "I'm sorry." I say, "I accept your apology," and then I grab the recipe. This happened on camera, we didn't rehearse it. She and I never had to discuss how we worked. She's very generous and so am I, so it was like a fusion.
Masterson: You have to have actors with stage experience for Horton's stuff. He writes a lot of dialogue. Fred Murphy would say, "I've never seen such long scenes." We'd do a take and it would be eight minutes long.
Glynn: I'd like to add to that because I cannot stress strongly enough how little money Pete had to do this project. He made it for one point six million dollars and shot it in 25 days. And it wasn't that long ago, in 1985. I bring that up because he couldn't

do big-bucks movie coverage, which is your master and then mediums and then two shots.

He'd design the way the entire scene moved and at what points he intended to cover it, because he didn't have time to cover the whole thing. So he needed actors that could play a 12-minute scene. That's never done in movies. You may get three pages shot if you're fast. So I really admired the way he did that.

Masterson: We had some days where we did 10 pages.

Glynn: If we didn't finish it we couldn't make the movie. There was no more money. So he had to do everything in the time allotted.

Do you think the limitation worked to your advantage?

Masterson: Sometimes it works for you and sometimes it works against you. For example, the scene Carlin mentioned, where Geraldine gives her the recipe back—I decided ahead of time to shoot that from the other room, looking in through the doors. I know that if I covered it I would have cut into it. But there are other times when I had to make a jump cut because I didn't want to wait for Geraldine and the sheriff to walk for a minute over to the other place. And everybody said, "Why did you do that?" And I said, "Because I don't have any coverage."

Glynn: He said, "Because I want the movie to move forward, I don't care if I look like a stupid director."

Can you talk about working together?

Masterson: We talk a lot off set. Actually, somebody said that after we'd been working on *Whorehouse* for awhile, they found out we were married.

What works for you professionally about knowing Pete so well and what doesn't?

Glynn: Well, his personality is such that he's a very calming influence, even when he is panicked. But I'd be aware. That's part of the positive, sensitive side of a relationship that becomes negative when you're working together. So even though I'm one of the cast, I can also see he's worried about losing the light. And it just so happened that I'd often be the last shot of the day, as the sun was going down. It would be my turn and I'd see Pete looking a little antsy, even though nobody knew that.

Masterson: Working with Carlin is very easy because she's just a very skillful actress. And she's helpful with other actors. She was with John [Heard].

Glynn: John is very confrontational. And he's like many very sensitive male artists—he has this exterior "fuck you, shock you" side. But I just ignored it and tried to get something going with him, because of the sexual aspect on the screen, which I felt had to underlie the relationship. So the first couple of weeks were really tough because he'd do dumb things, like talk dirty to try to shock me.

Masterson: John's an actor who'll eliminate everything. He'll say, "Why would I do that? Why don't I do this?" And that's the way he works, until he gets down to the only possible thing he can do, the thing he's supposed to do. We had this huge scene in the bus station in Houston, and I had planned out Ludie's and Jessie Mae's path when they come in. We got there in the morning and I even walked through it myself.

But when John got there he said, "Well, why would I do that?" I said, "Because that's where it lays out here." He said, "Yeah, but why don't I go over there first?" And I realized I'm ahead of myself. So I told him to do what he thought he should do. And he tried it out and about a half hour later he said, "I think you had it right in the first place." But he had to find it out for himself, just like all actors do. I know that, having been an actor myself. And in my haste to get this huge movie done in a short period of time I rushed things.

It sounds like you had to avoid being in an adversarial position with him.

Masterson: I never take that position with actors. There are directors who like that. Otto Preminger was famous for it. Ultimately things with John worked out. I just tried to relate to him as another human being, but it was not easy. Especially when he would say things like, "Why the fuck doesn't Jessie Mae get a job?" And I'd say, "Because in 1947 in Texas, it would be the ultimate emasculation of your character if you did not support your mother and your wife." Or one day he said, "Why can't Ludie be from Maryland instead of Texas?"

Glynn: Because John's from D.C.; he was worried about the accent.

Masterson: So I said, "Well, because people from Texas are polite, unlike people from Maryland." He started laughing.

He actually seemed very vulnerable in the movie.

Glynn: Well, that's the way he is. He's a wonderful actor. And as time passed it got easier.

Masterson: I loved working with him.

Pete, what was your favorite scene or scenes?

Masterson: The opening scene, which was not in the script. I made that up out of a monologue in the first scene, where Geraldine is telling Ludie about how she used to wake up in the night and take walks and the dogs would howl. I remember thinking, "Well, she's talking about when she was a young woman and had a little child." And I thought that would be nice —if we started the movie with some kind of romantic thing, some music. But the hard thing was that I did this all on the telephone.

Why?

Masterson: Because I was in New York and we wanted to shoot a bluebonnet field that was blooming down South. And with a small budget like we had, you couldn't afford to fly down there and back. Fortunately, the set and costume designers and cinematographer were down there. And they called me and said "You know, these bluebonnets are dying like mad."

I said, "Okay, get that girl who's going to be Geraldine's stand-in and dress her up in something that goes back 40 or 50 years." Then I told them to get a little boy to play John as a child, and I explained how they should do the scene. I told Fred to shoot it in slow motion and regular motion and different speeds and sizes and just have them run through the field. And I gave them some directing.

What was the result?

Masterson: Well, when I got down there, Fred said: "It's not any good. We got there too late and I didn't think we had enough light to shoot it in slow motion." When we got back to New York, I had some guys at the optical house take a look at it. One of them said he could blow it up in different sizes and start to pick out parts of it, and it would start to break up into little pieces. He went ahead, and it started to look like a pointillist painting.

How did you get it to look like it was in slow motion?
Masterson: You take out some frames and print each frame three to six times. Then I found this soprano to sing the hymn that Geraldine was singing in the opening. Horton didn't like it. He said, "This is not like Geraldine. She wouldn't sing like that." And I said, "Yeah, but she thinks she could. She remembers it that way."

So we went with the song. And it turned out he liked it. He also didn't want Geraldine to go into the house. That wasn't in the script. So I said, "I think that would be an interesting trip for her, if she goes in and walks around."

Why did you think of doing the opening that way?
Masterson: I kept thinking, how do we get into her mind and get the freedom of what it was before she was captured, caught in this place? So that's what I was looking for. As you segue out of that, into her singing, then you get the point. Otherwise we're in the room for 40 minutes before you get out. Then there's another musical sequence as soon as she leaves. That was all choreographed ahead of time.

We made one mistake. I was trying to get this scene to work, going from the opening sequence into the house, instead of it being a cut. I was going to have the crane move the camera closer and closer to the window until we go in the window and start the scene that way. We got out there at night, spent two hours getting everything ready and the crane wouldn't work. So I said: "Forget it. The shot's not worth it. Go home, guys."

Carlin, can you talk a little more about how you prepared for your role?
Glynn: I have a certain affinity for this character, so a lot of it was instinctual. I tried to look for the little girl in the character and therefore the little girl in myself. And I hate to say it, but it was not hard for me to do that. I have a real affinity for the sound and the language. As a young woman I was in Houston when the three movie theaters that Jessie talks about were there. So I had a sense of the place.

And though it wasn't always easy to work with John, I find him very attractive, so I could relate to him as a man. Also, there was one scene where I'm talking about my girlfriend and how she couldn't have a baby, which helped me get into my character.

In what sense?
Glynn: Well, not only was my friend childless, but so was I in the movie. That was part of Jessie Mae's subtext. It was one of the things that made her retain her childlike qualities, because she wasn't a parent. In a sense I love her because I think she's very valiant. She's an extremely unhappy woman who really refused to be so. She was going to dress up and go downtown to the movies and drugstore, and she was going to make her lists and make everything be okay. The important thing is not to create a character who has a negative impact on the audience.

So you have to get in touch with what you like about her?
Glynn: Right. And you have to find the justification for what she does. Nobody gets up in the morning and says, "I'm going to be a sonofabitch today." The women Horton writes are so rich. What he gives you and the places you have to go are so complex and fertile.

Do the props or set help you get there?
Glynn: Yes. As a matter of fact, Neil Spisak, the designer, asked us all what we wanted on the set, because every piece of furniture had personal objects in it. And I said I wanted a diaphragm put in the dresser, so that in rehearsal, when she goes to her dresser, she sees a sexual symbol. It was neat.

Did you know that, Pete? You look surprised.
Masterson: Yeah, I knew. But it was a surprise to Geraldine.
Glynn: That's why I did it. She didn't know it was in there. It was perfect. And then after she found out she just used the same reaction. We all worked using such intimate details. I had on underwear from the '40s. And I had this great walk in the movie, because I was wearing a tube girdle that costume designer Gary Jones got me.

Were the clothes made for you?
Glynn: No. They were all real clothes. They weren't built. They were found in basements out in Pennsylvania. For a period look, the hairdresser used only pin curls instead of hot rollers.

Were there any scenes that were difficult for you to play?

Glynn: Yes, the last part of the movie was really emotionally difficult for me as a person. And I wasn't aware of this until much later. I think it was because during the last period of the shooting I was the bad guy who was off in the car, or off in my honey wagon. Or I was the last one to get my hair done. I started to get paranoid and thought everybody hated me and I felt that Pete was being mean to me. But those feelings really informed the work toward the end of the movie.

How so?

Glynn: The truth is, Jessie Mae has been up all night. She's waiting in the car, while her husband and her rival are sitting on the porch of this old heap of a wreck of a house. So it paralleled the work, and there was a lesson in that. I always thought I was very good at not becoming the part I'm playing. But it taught me that I actually become very emotionally involved, even though I can leave the character and the accent behind. I remember carrying on when I had to run across the field because we were losing the light. I started screaming, "I'm never gonna forgive you again!"

Masterson: It actually was three pages of dialogue to get all the way across the field.

Glynn: So I'm feeling like everybody else got to act all day, and now that there's no time left, it's my turn! And as I'm starting this long walk across the field I see my fellow actor, John Heard, behind the camera reading a magazine. Well, I lost it! And he did not normally do this. He was usually a nice, generous actor off camera. So I just flipped out. And then I saw the daily and I said, "My God, she's such a shrew." And he said, "Yeah. It's perfect." All of that was going on so when Geraldine kissed me at the end, it just released a lot of stuff.

Were there scenes that you really enjoyed doing?

Glynn: I loved them all, and none of them was difficult technically. I liked walking down the street, or being in the beauty shop, or the drugstore, where you don't hear me say anything. Because I thought you saw another side of her—outside of that triangular relationship. You saw who she wanted to be. She wanted to have a nice day or buy a dress rather than being trapped in this situation. I love the last scene. I like walking up to the house mad having my list of rules. I like my shoes, and feeling thirsty. There are so many turns, from coming in with a lot of anger to trying to really work this out and make sure I get the rules out, to being kissed, or trying to recover, to being left out again. I like all that a lot.

Can you each talk about the role of the unconscious in your work?

Glynn: I don't understand the question. I mean, what would you say is the unconscious?

Your intuitive side.

Masterson: I don't know what I do unconsciously. I think it affects how you make choices, why you do this project or that project. When you write you never know where it comes from. I'll write a scene sometimes and I'll think, "Well, how did I write that scene?"

Do you feel you're open to that unknown territory?

Masterson: Yes. I nurture it and I try not to make too many plans. You have ground rules, but then you allow things to happen. Like when you act, you have certain things you're trying to accomplish, but you try to leave time for the unconscious.

Do you feel like it ever gets in your way?

Masterson: You can't allow that because then you become a plot writer, which does not inform your life. And that's OK, but that's not the business I'm in.

What about your work, Carlin, in terms of the unconscious?

Glynn: Well, first I pick the externals for the character, which is what she wears, how she walks and, in this instance, the accent. But once I've done my homework I would say that my unconscious controls my work. I really listened to that voice absolutely in terms of discovering elements in Jessie Mae's character and in her relationship with her husband.

Masterson: I like to plan the shots, and then you have to leave yourself open to having a better idea—if something comes to you or something comes to one of the actors. As a director, dealing with the unconscious also has to do with allowing other people's unconscious to work. It's part of the Method work we do at the Actors Studio, which helps you get to that basic instinct. That's why the relaxation exercises are so important, because nothing can happen with tension.

Glynn: In a way this work helps you tune your instrument, which as an actor is yourself, so you can leave it totally alone. I don't think some of the moments Geraldine and I had, like with the recipe or the kiss, would have happened without the kind of training we had at the Studio.

Were most of the actors in the film members of the Studio?

Glynn: Mostly everyone except John and Rebecca. People just don't realize what it takes to be an actor. You can't just say I'm a lawyer, but often people will say: "I'm an actor." I teach a class at Columbia where I show directors how to work with actors. One of my students is a well-known documentary filmmaker who's going to direct her first feature film. She's been given to me because she's never dealt with actors before. So I am trying to teach her how an actor approaches things, and she's got four months to do it in.

We take a lifetime to hone the craft. In rehearsal once Geraldine talked about a student she had who said, "Well, Miss Page, I'm going to do this for six months and if I haven't gotten it I'm gonna quit." And she said, "Why don't you quit right now!" Acting is a way of life. It's usually not a living.

Carlin, what about playing the madam in *Best Little Whorehouse*?

Glynn: I felt very strongly that I didn't want to do anything to glorify prostitution. But I also wanted to look at this as a business and the human side of it. It was very exciting to create a part, because you had input on what they were writing. And I think we all felt the same way.

Which was what?

Glynn: It wasn't a show about whoring. It's a very funny and political show and the madam is really a very maternal figure. I remember a woman outside the stage door one day, an older woman in a print dress and that blue kind of hair. She came up to me and said "Miss Glynn, I know exactly how you feel, I'm a house mother at Rutgers." And I just thought that was perfect. So that process was very different from *Bountiful*, where I was doing a role that had already been played by Kim Stanley, Eileen Hackert and Jo Van Fleet in the play version.

Did the fact that those other actresses had played the role affect your work?
Glynn: No, I was just flattered to be in that company. I didn't want to know how they worked on it. But creating a part in a play out of a whole story was the essence of the creative experience.

Can you talk a little bit more about working together as a married couple?
Masterson: Well, we usually discuss the motivation for the characters when we get home at night.
Glynn: Or in rehearsal with other actors. I think the basic thing is that Pete and I are trained in the same way. So there's a basic respect for the way we each work and there's a lot of shorthand sometimes. Of course, there are also arguments.

Such as?
Glynn: The toughest time for me is when he knows something and I can't get it. He thinks that because I'm married to him I should get it very rapidly. And then I get my feelings hurt.
Masterson: Maybe I'm a little more impatient with you than I am with other actors.
Glynn: Yeah, he really is. And I'm very quick, too. I work with facility and speed. So I get my feelings very hurt, because sometimes I think he treats everyone else better.
Masterson: It's probably true.
Glynn: But I surprise myself at how I can scream at my husband in front of a lot of people. It happens rarely, if ever; but I don't feel like I can't yell or that if I did he'd be mad at me when I got home.

Do you bring your baggage from rehearsal home with you?
Glynn: I think so. But you know it's work and you try to sort it out in the workplace. But I remember during the last period of *Bountiful*, I told John I was mad at Pete and I said, "Am I overreacting?" and he said "You sure are." And that was very helpful. Usually we're very good together.

Because you have a similar sensibility?
Glynn: Yes, and we like the same things. I'm more interested in personal or independent films than I would ever be in TV, or commercial film. I'm not saying that a commercial film can't also be a good film, but I love theater because it provokes people, and I think that commercial film and television have stopped trying to be provocative, in the sense that *Bountiful* is.

Another thing that works for us is the way Pete runs his set. Whether it's theater or film, he has as much respect for his gaffer or his grip as he does for his stars. People are polite to each other and they respect one another.

How has your work changed over time?
Masterson: It's easier, because you get smarter, hopefully. It's not that the problems are more easily solved, but the process of directing is something I know more about. You can't take any shortcuts; but I guess one of the things I have learned is not to do all the talking. I used to give long lectures about the backgrounds of the characters and the situation, and now everybody is part of the discussion. The more I expose the actors and the designers and everybody else to the material and the more we discuss it, the more they come to it on their own terms and they feel like they thought of it—and maybe they did.

So you listen to people more.
Masterson: Yes. In a film you have a lot of departments, so you have to listen. You do in a musical, too. Working on *Whorehouse* made it easier for me to do a film, because I was used to working with a lot of different departments—the sound department or the lighting department or the music department or the choreographers. In a film it's similar. You just replace the choreographer with the cinematographer.

You get different things from each of the talents?
Masterson: Yes. I find the designers have input into things that the actors don't. The designers have their own method. I did a film called *Full Moon in Blue Water*. Gene Hackman has a house and he's looking at movies of his dead wife. And the designer said, "Who brought the furniture into this house? Was it his wife, or did he have this here before he married her? How long were they married? Is this her taste or his taste?" So we called

the writer, and we started talking about it.

Did that happen with *Bountiful*?

Masterson: Yes. *Bountiful* was supposed to take place in 1952. I changed it to 1947 because I liked the design better. The clothes were more interesting, the colors were more interesting. There was a big change after that. They had the new look, which took place around '49 when the women's skirts dropped way down. So we went back to '47 with the suits, and the spectators' shoes and hats.

Glynn: *Bountiful* was an absolute creative collaboration, with everybody pulling for the same thing, nobody being treated any differently than anyone else. But the goal was the product in every area. The crew even offered to give Pete free time on a movie. He refused, but for them to offer to work for nothing is unheard of. I guess what we've addressed pretty much is not only personal creativity but collaborative creativity. And that informed both *Bountiful* and *Whorehouse*.

Masterson: It might not seem that a big musical about a whorehouse and *Trip to Bountiful* had much in common, but they're both about place, and an invasion of space somehow by something else, and I think they're both personal stories.

> ❛ I'm always making mental notes about things. You have a real thought and then your imagination takes over and the thought is changed. ❜

HORTON FOOTE
Screenwriter

As the interview began in his Greenwich Village apartment, Horton Foote was very much the Southern gentleman with an air of reserve. But a twinkle came to his eyes once he began talking about his characters. Just the mention of Scout, the young girl in his adaptation of *To Kill a Mockingbird*, or Mrs. Watts, a part that won Geraldine Page an Academy Award in *The Trip to Bountiful*, and Foote was in the comfortable company of memorable stage and screen characters from his own pen.

Foote, known for his character-driven stories, saw his work first pro-

Horton Foote: "*Bountiful* has been a teleplay, a play and then a screenplay with different casts each time."

duced on Broadway in 1944, when he was only 28. He wrote the original version of *The Trip to Bountiful* for TV, then turned it into a stage play, and finally a screenplay—without sacrificing his unique ear for dialogue.

His script from Harper Lee's novel, *To Kill a Mockingbird*, won him an Academy Award in 1961. He admits to having felt somewhat apprehensive about this project because away from the stage he had adapted only one novel and two Faulkner stories, "The Old Man" and "Tomorrow," for TV's *Playhouse 90*. Two years after *Mockingbird* he wrote another classic, *Baby, the Rain Must Fall*, and in 1979 he began work on another film which would earn him his second Academy Award, *Tender Mercies*.

Though Foote keeps an apartment in Manhattan with his wife, Lillian, he likes to return to his Southern roots. Born in Wharton, Texas, he still resides there part of the year. Like Mrs. Watts in *Bountiful*, Foote says he feels cut off if he doesn't go back.

You once said you tried to begin *The Trip to Bountiful* with the day Geraldine Page's character, Mrs. Watts, was to be married—but it didn't work. Why was that?

I don't know why. Actually I really wanted to do a story about a woman who couldn't marry the man she loved and was forced to marry someone else under very particular circumstances. So that's when I tried to start it on the day of the wedding, and it just didn't work. I think it's just a question of the material asserting itself in a certain kind of way. Sometimes you have to be very patient and sometimes it tells you right away. I've learned not to force things. If it's not going to work, it's not going to work. So I backed away, and then it just came to me to start it at a whole different place, at the end of her life.

And that's where the film starts now.

Right. And actually that incident where this woman couldn't marry a certain man became a very minor thing that she referred to on the bus.

When did you start working on *Bountiful*?

Actually it was in the early days of television, when television was live and there was a wonderful producer named Fred Coe who fashioned his programs on the writer. He commissioned us, and all we had to do was tell him just the briefest of ideas. But I was not able to do that. I always had to write the whole thing out.

And so *Bountiful* started as a teleplay.
Yes. And then it became a play. The shows that I was writing for TV were just one hour, and they were nearer to one-act plays. I had a lot of those stored up, so they were already written in a way.

You said that you were not able to tell the producer your ideas. Why was that?
I guess I've always resisted cooperative writing in a way. I mean in the sense of everybody giving their ideas, and everybody saying let's try this and let's try that. You get away from the source, I think. I've always resisted that way of working, not out of arrogance, but I've just had some kind of deep sense that the writer knows what he's doing.

Did you like working for TV?
Well, it was hard because it was live and it was very restrictive. And so you could never really take the journey. *Bountiful* has been a teleplay, a play and then a screenplay with different casts each time.

How did it change?
Each cast brings something intangible, but it's enormous. If you have good actors and you have actors of integrity, then you just go with them. The results are very different and the difference has to do with the nature of the talent and the instrument of each actor.

One of Geraldine Page's lines has stayed with me over the years. It goes something like, "I'm only 12 miles away..."
"I've come this far, I'm only twelve miles..."

What works about that line is that a woman's whole lifetime is condensed into one line. It's so specific and yet so many people write so generally.
I just don't know what's happening to writing—it's getting very abstract. And it goes beyond reality, I think. At least with

writers that I like. They have a sense of place, and I don't mean that you're confined by that. When you deal with it, you deal with it very specifically. It's like acting. You have to be very specific in acting as far as I'm concerned. All this new acting is so vague and general and people come up with caricatures.

Is that something that comes naturally to you, to write that specifically?

As a writer you kind of seek your level, and you instinctively know what's good for you and other writers. I think the writers I admire do that.

Who do you admire?

Well, you go through stages. Right now I admire the wonderful short stories of Flannery O'Connor. And Elizabeth Bishop, of course. She just staggers you with those kinds of details that just reverberate and do all kinds of things.

There was a critic who once said your work was small. And you responded: "It's not small, it's personal." How do you get to that intimate place?

I was trained as an actor. I think that's part of why it's natural for me to get to those personal places you're talking about. It's almost like an acting exercise, where you don't recall the emotion—you recall the events around the emotion. And as a writer that's what I always did, recall the events so that I could bring back certain feelings. That kept my imagination going.

Can you think of any specific examples?

Well, no, it's just that when I'm working on something I try to re-create a particular moment or time. I use my imagination and I try to remember what a day was like or what the room was like.

Your hometown is Wharton, Texas, right?
Yes.

And that seems to affect your work.

Yeah, I guess it does. I think it's a privilege to grow up in the South. There's a whole tradition and there are vivid stories there. I do think there's a sense of belonging to something. I do not mean to be indulgent about this, but as a Southerner you have a certain perspective or feeling about things.

Do you believe in using material from your past?
Yes, but I don't think you should be restricted to that. I think the present is important.

I think it was Frank Rich who said your work was turbulent beneath a tranquil surface.
I guess so. He's been very good to my work.

Has he said anything that has helped you?
His observations are helpful. You always want people to respect and admire your work. When you read what they say about it, you say, "I don't know if that was what I specifically intended to do but it's very helpful to know how it's perceived." I think even negative criticism can be helpful. Once in a while you realize you have to make something clearer.

Frank Pierson said Al Pacino almost dropped out of *Dog Day Afternoon* until Pierson made certain changes in the script. Have you encountered that kind of situation with an actor?
Well, no, I don't usually have such an adversarial position. Usually they're quite supportive. Sometimes they make suggestions. At one point I wanted to do another rewrite of *Tender Mercies*. Someone said to me, I think there should be an older person, and that just started a whole different track of thinking. I was grateful for that.

Do you often have a very strong vision?
I'm stubborn, if that's what you mean. I know pretty well whether I've achieved what I want to achieve. I've also lived long enough to know that sometimes it takes time for things to be appreciated.

It was written that a turning point in your life was when your grandfather died. Is that true?
Yes, in a way. But I wasn't conscious of that when I was writing. It was a certain time in my life when this man was dead and the whole world changed—there was a different set of values

and a protective feeling that I had. Life was very temporary.

Do you think that that feeling entered into your works?
I think it enters into everything I write about. I think everything's about change or the mystery of change. Or the result of change.

Do you feel that writing is very unconscious?
Yes.

What helps you find that place in yourself?
I don't know. I love to write. I have no desire except to bring order to the things that interest me. And that really is the basic gift. I've been fortunate to make some kind of living and feed my children and do all those things that one expects to do in life. But that's never been the goal for me. My family's been good about that.

It sounds like your unconscious is very accessible to you.
I guess it is. I'm at work now and I find myself getting more and more isolated and more withdrawn. I think it's just going into a world that I like to go into. I don't know where I'm going yet. It's kind of uncharted. I always like the journey.

Does it frighten you at all?
Not really. I just like to go there.

In *Bountiful* the characters are so sympathetic and clearly defined. How were you able to accomplish that?
I just tried to find, in that given situation, what type of characters would be there.

By "situation" do you mean an unemployed man living with his wife and his mother in a small house down South?
Yes. And once you understand the situation they're in it's not hard to feel sympathetic. I don't think anyone is really unsympathetic if you know enough about them. I think you can forgive almost anyone. It's lack of knowledge that makes us dislike people.

Can you talk about how you started working on
Mockingbird?
It was 25 years ago, and I remember it being a happy time. I
was used to doing my own stuff. I really don't like adapting
other people's work. But my wife read Harper Lee's novel and
said, "You better read this." I had met Harper, who didn't want
to do the movie. So I decided to do it.

Did you relate to the material?
Well, yes. It took place in a town I knew in Georgia. It was like
the town I grew up in.

Was it hard to transform the novel into a film?
At first. But several things helped me. One was a review I
read by R.P. Blackmur, called "Scout in the Wilderness." He com-
pared Scout with Huck in *Huckleberry Finn.*

How so?
He talked about the hypocrisy in a small Southern town, seen
through the point of view of the children. And he said in both
novels we discover the hypocrisy along with the children.
Another thing that helped me was when Alan Pakula, who was
the producer, said we had to change Harper's fine structure.
And if we hadn't, we would have killed ourselves.

How did you change the structure?
He said that the events that took place over several years
could be condensed into one year. That was freeing to me. The
other thing that helped me was when I found out that the character of Dill was based on Truman Capote.

But essentially you kept many of the scenes from the novel.
Oh yes. But I had to invent different scenes as well. For
instance, there was never any mention of the mother. And so I
invented that little scene where Scout asks her father and brother
about her mother.

Did you base anything on your own childhood?
Well, when we were growing up my parents used to sit on the
porch. My bedroom was off the porch and I used to hear everything they said, and so that's why I put certain scenes in where

the kids listen to everything.

And everyone thought they had something of an Atticus in their father.

What was your favorite scene?
At the end of the movie when Scout says, "Hey Boo," when he's hiding behind the door.

The mob scene was a stand-out.
That was a difficult scene—to write, act and direct—to believe that Scout could turn the mob around. You have to really believe in the girl.

What about *Tender Mercies*?
I had been working on a cycle of plays and I'd run out of money and my agent said I should do a film. I just went home and went to work and wrote it and felt it was a wonderful part for Bob [Robert Duvall]. We tried to do it ourselves, but we couldn't get the money.

Do you prefer plays to films?
I don't know what I prefer. I think I'd hate to stop either one.

Do you enjoy the limitations of a play?
You just have to adjust to that. They're two different forms. I'm not a conventional filmmaker. I just think language is important. Films are getting to be more like MTV. People get very nervous when they hear all my dialogue in a film. But that's my style.

Who gets nervous?
Hollywood people.

How has your work changed over time?
I don't know if it has changed—it's just developed and matured. I think there are things I did as a young writer that I couldn't do now. Once the thing is written, you go on. The mistake writers make is that they keep repeating themselves. I'm inclined to believe that what you write about is set for you almost like a computer—when you're 12 years old. I don't think that's true for every writer. But it is for anyone I feel an affinity

for and for myself. It doesn't mean that you write what you felt when you were 12; but that's what you focus on.

And your focus was on the South.
That's just the place. It's deeper than that—it's what's in you, how you perceive that material.

What kind of characters interest you?
I'm just interested in people.

Nick Kazan said that being a writer is like being a receptacle of sorts. Do you feel that, too?
I suppose I do. I receive it and then I meditate—I walk and think a great deal. But I don't walk so much here in New York.

Can you talk about your process?
Walking and thinking. Someone said that Hawthorne thought out every word before he wrote *The Scarlet Letter*. The novel has the feeling of walking.

Does walking help you clear your mind?
Not clear your mind so much as it helps you focus somehow. You get to thinking.

In a more creative way?
Right. Some people need to create a crisis to do their work. I don't need to do that. I really need to be left alone. I need to get out and go back and forth.

Someone wrote that you like to write in longhand and that you keep notebooks. And once you get going the writing takes over and you wake up in the middle of the night...
That's right. I'm also always making mental notes about things. You have a real thought and then your imagination takes over and the thought is changed.

Do you get lonely when you're writing?
I never feel lonely.

Do you read your stuff aloud?
Not when I'm writing, but maybe later when I'm working on

it. I like to script the whole thing and then bring it to the actors.

Do you work certain hours?
I wish I could say I was disciplined. I'm not. I'm really an obsessive writer. Sometimes I get up in the middle of the night and get to work. I'm not an 8-to-10 man or an 8-to-12 writer like Hemingway was.

Has that been hard on your family?
My children are all grown and my wife is so used to it. I think probably at one time they felt I was insensitive to them.

Who has had the biggest influence on you?
As a writer, my wife.

And you take what she says to heart.
Sure do. She's very supportive. I'll ask her questions and I'll have to draw her out on certain things that I'm insecure about.

Are there directors or actors that you like working with?
Oh, Lord, I've had so many. I love working with Pete [Masterson] and Carlin [Glynn].

Because they understand your work.
Yes, I think so. I think they've been trained the way I was as an actor—at the Actors Studio. I love working with Herbert [Berghof]. Lots of people.

And you said that your training as an actor has helped you.
I think so. You learn to break down a piece and tear it apart.

Do you get blocked at all?
Not consciously. I always have a number of things I'm thinking about, and if something's not working I just put it aside for a while and start something. I don't believe in just fixing something.

Does New York inspire you or do you prefer the South?
Well, I also live in New Hampshire and that's where I work regularly. I'm very isolated here in New York; I can shut myself

off here. I was never able to write in the South until the last 10 years.

Why is that?
I don't know. I think the reality was so overwhelming that I had to get away from it and think about it.

Some people advocate writing about what you know best and some people say you need a certain distance. What do you think?
I think it depends on the circumstances. Faulkner stayed in the South. And then you have Katherine Anne [Porter], who's as specific as you can get, but she wandered all over the world and never went back South. And look at Joyce: He lived in Dublin and Paris. And Gertrude Stein. You just can't make rules about those things.

Personally I had to always go back. Otherwise I'd feel cut off—I needed to watch. But there's a lot of energy in New York. Part of me wishes the theater was more alive in New York. I was in London for two years. What a difference.

Does that affect you—the change in theater?
You just have to go on and say it's temporary.

What are your strengths and your weaknesses?
I don't think about that. You just plow on. I just think you have to try and keep in touch with yourself and find out what's best for you.

You talked about writers nowadays writing in general terms. Why do you think that is?
Most of it is because we get interested in what we think are themes and in generalities and in trying to make comments, rather than letting life make the comment.

❝ The days of being the mad designer in the costume room with the sketch pad, demanding that the silk chiffon be flown in from Paris, is not the way it works anymore. More often than not, it's about discovering the right pair of Jockey briefs. ❞

GARY JONES
Costume Designer

Gary Jones's office in Manhattan is filled with racks of costumes that have been worn or will be worn in some of our best-known plays and movies, including *Hair, A Chorus Line, Bonfire of the Vanities, Best Little Whorehouse* and *The Trip to Bountiful.*

After leaving Ohio University, Jones migrated to Manhattan, where he joined the New York Shakespeare Festival. The time was 1967 and the festival, otherwise known as the Public Theatre, was an exciting place to be. Jones stayed 10 years, designing costumes for all three versions of *Hair,* which found its origins there. His last show at the Public was *A Chorus Line,* which he followed to Broadway.

He soon met the woman who would change the course of his career—teacher, mentor and collaborator Anne Roth. Jones and Roth were designing costumes for the movie version of *Hair* when Tommy Tune called to say he was working on a musical with a director named Pete Masterson. Roth and Jones had their hands full, but accepted an offer to join the project—*Best Little Whorehouse.*

The show ran for several years. Jones became close with Masterson, Carlin Glynn, the star of the show, and Neil Spisak, the set designer. So when those three began collaborating on another project, it seemed only natural for Masterson to call Jones.

Thus he joined the *Trip to Bountiful* collaboration.

Trip to Bountiful **was an extraordinary picture. What created the magic?**

One of the things that was so thrilling about that project from the very beginning was the literature. It was there. And then Pete gathered together this incredible group of people. And when I eventually met Horton I understood, in a way, some sort of legacy of the integrity of the piece.

I read the play and the screenplay and then looked at a lot of pictures of the play and from that we set out with a whole other idea, which was basically Edward Hopper. And it then got a little bit into Andrew Wyeth, too. It was Americana without being kitschy; but it was a bold American sort of statement that Pete wanted to make.

Do you remember who came up with the idea of Hopper?

It's funny because it really is the old chicken-and-egg question. I'm not sure who first said the word "Hopper." But when it was established that we would be using the bold style of Hopper I thought of his painting of a diner, which is lighted so you can see inside at nighttime. Two or three people are sitting there and the red dress that Jessie Mae wears comes from that. I don't know if the dress in the diner is red, but there is a color in the diner that brought all of this together for me.

Can you talk more about that?

As I recall, in a Hopper painting the woman is usually the bright color. In fact, she is the light in the painting. The men wear brown and gray. No man would have worn a vibrant yellow shirt in his right mind. And so it does all add up to Jessie Mae, the woman of the piece.

What do you focus on when you're first beginning a movie?

The character. There are always so many considerations in a given movie, but what I know to be the truth is that I can only work from the character. I cannot accommodate a television personality and be happy with what I'm doing.

Why is that?

Because our job is to tell a story that is prescribed by the literature that it comes from. I'm not saying there's anything wrong with being a TV personality. But if you have someone who says,

Carlin Glynn in *Bountiful*. Says Gary Jones of the character Jessie Mae: "She was drawn to the movie magazines, and that's where her sense of style came from.

"The wardrobe lady at CBS told me I can't wear yellow," already we're in trouble. That doesn't mean I want yellow, but it means that I'm dealing with a limited consciousness about how far you might have to go to get this right. And it's very difficult to work that way.

And you didn't have that kind of limitation in *Bountiful*?

No, there was an incredible commitment to the piece and to both Horton and Pete. And Pete was steadfast in supporting Neil, the scenery designer, and myself. The feeling was, "This is the direction we want to take, and these are the people who are taking us there, and within whatever boundaries or limitations there are, let's go with them."

And so there was no back-pedaling like, "Well, maybe you don't have to wear a girdle because it's not comfortable." Unfortunately in 1947 unless you were working in the fields or you were pregnant, you had on a bra and a girdle and hose if you went out.

Can you talk about what your vision was with each character?

I'm probably better at some people than others. But once you get a couple of key people going, then it becomes a rhythm and a very natural thing so you can start collecting ideas and fabrics which eventually get used and add up to something. Another thing about the *Bountiful* experience, which was rare, is that Pete gave us the luxury of choosing the style and carrying it through completely.

What did that mean to your own work?

It means really committing to something. People often say they just "want something to look real"—which means they don't know what they want it to look like. If you want to cover a screen in red, for instance, or have someone walk onto a screen in red, you have to be committed to having something feel red.

So what questions would you ask yourself?

Take Jessie Mae's red dress. You have to understand where that came from, why she selected it, what she was thinking, how much it cost, did she make it herself, would she have known to make it herself? Those are the questions you ask. That's really the way we work and I find that it benefits everyone.

Do you relate to the time period of the movie?

Well, I have always had an affinity for the clothes right around that period from '47 to, let's say, '54. And yet, I was born in '47 so I have no formal memory of the clothes. But they're in some part of my memory.

Which part?
The feeling of the clothes. I don't remember the specific coats my mother wore, but they had a certain feeling. I never saw my mother in a suit, for instance, but I knew they existed and I knew what they looked like. So it was very wonderful when I realized that Pete wanted to start in 1947 and go from there.

What about John Heard's character? What did you concentrate on?
John was really a great joy to work with. We were able to accomplish one of the most successful male looks of the period on him. I think that happened because he relaxed into it. He accepted the fact that men wore shirts and ties, period, and he really got into it. It really was a great triumph because I totally believed him as a not-so-successful business person, but someone who was trying.

Did you ever disagree on his clothes?
Yes. He was not sure about his shirt because it was a fuller shirt than we are used to today, with slightly fuller sleeves. My recollection is that he thought it made him look heavier and the truth was that it made him look real and much more believable.
There was a hat he wanted to wear, but he wanted a wider brim than we had. So we got him the wider brim and I said, "Well, if you wear the hat in a certain place, give me the shirt." It was half a joke and half the truth. And he said, "Fine, it's a deal." And we both won. It's one of those very nice bargains.

He had this look of wanting to get somewhere but never quite making it.
Exactly. On so many levels he's a loser, but he's not really a loser in our sense of things today.

Meaning what?
Well, he isn't the strong man of this piece. He is the weakest of them all, in a way, and yet he is the man of the time.

And of this time too, because he was a sensitive character.

Yes. And he was trying to cope, which is much more the '90s kind of a man, interestingly enough, instead of the '70s or '80s.

But the clothes in the '90s are very different from that time period, aren't they?

I'm trying to think about the look of the '90s. I have a better feeling about women's clothes than I do about men's right at the moment. It is coming back to better workmanship, like it was back then.

What about Jessie Mae's look?

Jessie Mae I found fascinating—she was drawn to the movie magazines, and that's where her sense of style came from. It's where her earrings and her jewelry came from. And it's where the dress and shoes she wore, as she walked across the field, came from. I'm sure she saw the dress in some magazine, and then went out to buy a dress that was that dramatic. I would like to think it wasn't a dress that everybody in town had. She really wanted to be glamorous, and so her hair had a Rita Hayworth quality to it and her smoking had a movie-star quality to it.

Were the clothes real antique clothes or were they made for the actors?

I believe Jesse Mae's clothes were real. John's suit was real. His shirts were not, they were made. And I believe his hat was made. And Geraldine's clothes were made.

Who made the choices for Jessie Mae's wardrobe?

Everything she wore was something that I wanted her to wear. We danced around with other ideas. But these were our ultimate choices after a lot of searching. In many cases, especially with a period film, you have the right suit, but it's the wrong color. But in this particular case there was a lot of work done on those clothes.

What kind of work did you have to do?

Fitting. Carlin is tall. They required lengthening and/or shortening—basic alterations. But to do that on existing garments is a very delicate job—not so delicate in the theater, but in film everything has to be perfect. Fortunately, the actors wore their clothes well and it didn't seem like they were putting anything on. I will always see Jessie Mae with her dressing gown and her slippers, just sitting there smoking. Once we were on the set it looked exactly as I had imagined it would, every bit of it.

That's great, because sometimes you have to change your own vision.
Sometimes you have to change your vision and you have to help change theirs because something doesn't work on the set. I mean, we had a lot of jokes on *Trip to Bountiful* because God was the gaffer when we were out in those fields, and we had to wait until the light was right, period.

How were Geraldine's clothes affected by Hopper?
She relates to Hopper only in that she is the Earth. And Hopper, was in a way, the city. So she was the opposite of that. I had never known Geraldine, except we had met once at the New York Shakespeare Festival, socially. I had shopped for fabrics for her because I knew we would have to make her clothes and to have an extra one when she fell down. As I recall, we were look-ing at the fabrics in a costume house and the first thing out of Geraldine's mouth after we said hello was, "I just keep thinking about flowers." And as we looked down, there were a number of floral ideas there. Once again, the one that she wore was the one that I just simply loved—the gray dress with the little flowers. And that all really came from a very personal association I had.

Which was what?
Memories of both my grandmothers and the clothes they wore and the way they looked. Not that it was a direct transla-tion, but it was a feeling that they always had when they were working in their own homes.

Can you describe the feeling?
Well, the feeling for me was one of total comfort and work — providing for and caring, total mothering qualities. That was in the back of my mind. I recall making a funny drawing of the way I thought the top of that dress was. I never drew the bottom of the dress. And so we made the dress except for finishing its length. Geraldine came back for her second fitting, we put it on, marked the length and that was the end of the discussion.

Geraldine is the antithesis of the Hopper painting. She's nurturing and earthy, and the Hopper paintings always look like they need a mother. If you're thinking Hopper, how does that translate to Geraldine?

I was very clear that both were right. I do know that the flowers were very much in both of our minds. And Pete left us to our own, which is a great joy. He created an atmosphere where you didn't feel afraid to try things. Even if you only have three or four weeks, you still have time. There's a joke, "Jumbo by Monday." You know, a lot of ballets have been done between Friday and Monday and they are dancing on Monday night. So if you don't feel afraid to try and make a mistake, it's a lovely thing.

Do you think that by working with opposites, such as Geraldine and Hopper's work, you were able to find Geraldine's essence?

Absolutely. And once again I have to say that you start with the characters. Their voices were the first things that I heard. Then the Hopper paintings came and that gave a wonderful insight into what I call the city. Geraldine talked about getting out of the city—"leaving this city and that apartment." And whether it was a big city or a small city, an apartment does not mean country. So she was the opposite. Her heart was the opposite of Hopper, and therefore it went in that direction.

When you say you heard their voices, what did you hear?

In reading the script, you hear the words that she chooses, as opposed to the words that Jessie Mae uses, which are quick and harsh and city words. They're not just young, they are city. She's not the younger version of Geraldine.

She seems older than Geraldine.

Absolutely. But she is very different. Geraldine is as simple as the dirt that she touches at the end. That was what remained throughout her life. And that also connected very much with both of my grandmothers, who were incredibly strong women, who remained exactly what they were throughout the Depression and through World War II. And, in fact, my grandmother, I think, died the year that movie was released.

Where were your grandmothers from?

My family is from Ohio. So they have a different background than Geraldine's character, but they really shared something. They were all women of the Earth in one way or another.

There's a lot of love you obviously have for your grandmothers. Do you feel that you brought that to your work with Geraldine?

Absolutely. There's a lot of love in that whole project. And it's with the people involved and the literature and it just continues to build. Pete must have told you that we had terrible budgetary problems. I mean, to save five cents the hairdresser was sent away the day before a closeup. That kind of nonsense.

What happens if someone doesn't get your vision?

I'm not very good at arguing a point. This may be very much to my detriment, but I feel, "If you don't get the picture, you don't get the picture." It's not that I don't want to take the time really, it's that I don't quite know how to get it across to you. If you don't understand why Geraldine needs X, Y, and Z, I'm already on to the next thing. And quite honestly I've usually ordered both dresses and they're on their way.

Did budget problems get in the way of your realizing your vision?

Definitely. Both Neil Spisak and I fought to get the things we thought were necessary—just to have the crew that we needed and the equipment that was needed, and it was all a labor of love. I recall sitting on these terrible couches in a condo and saying, "We really need X, Y and Z, otherwise, we can't do this tomorrow." I had never done that before. I had never fought for what I wanted or for a visual sense I had.

Why were you able to for this movie?

I felt people were on my side and I felt that we were all doing the same movie. And that we had done the best we could within the budget and therefore they were going to have to stretch a little bit, too. It was not a matter of buying fur coats for people and that kind of excess of the movie business. This was getting it done, treating people nicely, graciously. Geraldine needed a certain amount of tending to, for instance.

What about Rebecca De Mornay?

The sweet young thing. The one thing I remember about Rebecca, whom I had worked with just before in a movie called *The Slugger's Wife*, is that she looked at the girdle as though it were some sort of alien creature and I was tempted to make fun. But then I handed her stockings and I saw how she had no idea how to operate a garter. Her mother did not have to wear them, the way my mother did, which is how I knew about such things. But at any rate, I knew very early on about undergarments and she did not know, and there was something lovely about her innocence. So we sat down and discussed how you get a seam up the back and then we had a lesson about how to walk and how the girdle changes your posture.

Did you see her change?

It was thrilling because by the end of the hour she got the picture and she understood how it felt. But she didn't like it at first because a girl of the '80s, who is free and clear and braless, has a very different feeling. But she really did get it.

What specifically do you think she realized?

That the innocence that she needed was something different than just the sweet young thing. It was a very deep-seated and moral issue, the innocent part of this role. I mean a woman, or anyone in 1947, doesn't know what we know. A 10-year-old now knows more than that woman knew at 20 or 25 or whatever she was supposed to be. And that woman will never know what we know now by the time you're 50. And would never have to deal with any of those issues.

You were starting to say that by wearing the clothes, that's how she knew about the deep-seated innocence.

Well, I think so and I could see her change as she looked in the mirror. I could see her going inside. It wasn't instant; it happened during that first hour.

Can you talk about your relationship with the other creative forces—like Horton Foote?

The great thing about Horton is that he has a wonderful memory and his characters are all alive for him. But I didn't talk to him much about *Bountiful*. My sense was that he liked everything we did but he wasn't around a lot. He came to Texas and visited us but he had two other scripts being shot that summer, so he was going from place to place.

What were the most memorable conversations that you had?
Two funny things happened. One was a conversation I had with Neil Spisak about the fact that we would use all solid colors, which I took to mean blocks of color, or strength of color, rather than just flat color. But I think Neil meant no print fabrics. In the movie we used all print fabric but the colors were solid.

The other thing I recall was that I had a rack of endless clothes that I was trying to sort out and a tiny rack of the principals' clothes which had been delivered from New York. I showed it to Fred Murphy, who was the director of photography, and he said that he thought maybe Rebecca De Mornay's coat was a little too green. I said, "Yes," and I never thought about it again. I was very committed to that coat. And then I noticed that the walls in the apartment were green. But I never once mentioned the coat, nor did he, and it all matched. It was of the right time and so it worked.

I remember those two instances because they are about how it gets done and what the steps are for each department. And as sure as I'm sitting here, Neil Spisak meant solid blocks of solid color. But in a way, it wasn't what I heard.

Do you remember any conversations you had with Pete?
Pete falls in love with his characters. I would say things like, "Is this a woman who gets out of bed in the morning and stays in her nightgown until one, two, three in the afternoon, smoking? Or does she go to work?" Or we'd talk about how she spends her day getting herself together. We don't know quite for what, because obviously their sex life isn't so hot.

The only things she gets herself ready for are her trip to the beauty parlor, and her trip to the Coca Cola place, the drugstore. Those are the kinds of things we talk about. And I also had to remind Pete that men always wear shirts and ties and that farmers are definitely farmers. They were very clear in their roles. For instance, a businessman would never wear blue jeans. Those kinds of definitions were very clear, up until the middle '50s.

You said that one of the few things Jessie Mae gets herself

ready for is a trip to the beauty parlor. They all seem to be getting ready for things they'd like to have. Lootie's getting ready for a job that he's not really going to, and Geraldine is getting ready to go to a home that's no longer hers and Jessie Mae is probably getting ready for a sex life she doesn't have.

Exactly. Because they're all people who didn't have a lot. And yet Jessie Mae certainly had pretense to other things, through her movies, and there was a bit of what I call the facade of that period.

Meaning?

You know, that business of everything being in the dumper, but your father wouldn't tell you that you didn't have any money. I never knew how much money my father made until the day he died. But you looked good, you kept it together, you did not tell the neighbors, and this is all about not letting anybody know. That was the American family in a way.

Which ties into what you said before about Andrew Wyeth affecting your work.

That's right. The last shot, of her looking back at the house, is sort of *Christina's World.* The colors were much more Edward Hopper—the vibrancy of the sky and the green of the field was very clearly the Hopper influence, but the Americana of the Wyeth world was definitely there.

You said that when you're shopping you may not even know what you're getting, but you'll see something that will spark you.

There were a number of fabrics. Quite honestly the fabric of Carlin's robe—I knew I was going to use it. And I found Geraldine's purse and hat very late in the game. But I put my hands on the hat and I knew that it was the right one. I bought two. I had a feeling about that hat. And the minute she put it on there was no question.

And you also knew the purse would be for her?

Yes. And that I bought very early on. Actually I knew the purse was for her because it was too old for Jessie Mae. And I suppose the other side of that is that if it hadn't worked for Geraldine some extra could have carried it. The strange thing is,

I don't really know any other way to do it, whether I have $10,000, which is what I think that budget was, or whether the budget was as large as *Bonfire of the Vanities*. I always start by finding things that get these characters moving.

Do you remember the first thing you bought for *Bountiful*?
I remember buying a bunch of slips and undergarments and nightgowns and that gave me a feeling of where I was. We started at the bottom when we did Shakespeare in the Park. We made everybody's corsets, underwear and bloomers.

So that's why you got into the feeling of it when you bought the nightgowns.
Yes, I'm sure that's one of the connections. And also, having a real background as a dressmaker, I hold onto fabrics. Especially when I see one that I like. It often sits right back here throughout the production and then, at some moment, I'll grab it and say, "Let's make a bow tie out of this."

Can you talk about working with Ann Roth?
Sure. We've worked together for nearly 15 years. Our first movie was *Hair*. It has been an extraordinary journey for both of us, I would be so bold as to say. And totally joyous for me.

Ann has encouraged my solo career more than anyone in the world, and I love our work together because it is such a collaboration.

What are the most important things that you've learned from her?
How important your instincts and perceptions of people are. Because a lot of this is about dealing with people, just like every business. Film people like to think it's special—it's not. I'm sure if you work at an ad agency you have to deal with people, too, or American Express or anyplace else. But it is about those personalities.

The days of being the mad designer in the costume room with the sketch pad, demanding that the silk chiffon be flown in from Paris, is not the way it works anymore. More often than not, it's about discovering the right pair of Jockey briefs. Like the movie I'm doing now—*East of Eden*, which Sidney Lumet is directing— finding the right pair of briefs became important. Not in a sexual way, but to give a sense of reality because they might be seen when the character undresses.

What is the greatest challenge you face in your work?
Making people look their best within their character. That doesn't mean they're perfect. I love when people aren't perfect—when their tie is askew.

❝ We were on a tight budget. And, of course, a favorite thing that producers like to say is, 'Oh, it will stimulate your creativity, you'll have to come up with other ways of doing it.' That's one take on it. Sometimes that does happen and sometimes it doesn't. ❞

NEIL SPISAK
Production Designer

The man who contributed much to the detailed, authentic look of time and place in *The Trip to Bountiful* has a long list of production credits, both in theater and film. After earning his BFA in scenery and costume design from Carnegie-Mellon University in 1978, Neil Spisak assisted costume designer Ann Roth on such films as *The Morning After, Sweet Dreams, Jagged Edge, Places in the Heart, Silkwood, The World According to Garp* and *Dressed to Kill.* He also assisted Roth on numerous Broadway productions, including *Social Security, House of Blue Leaves, Present Laughter* and *The Misanthrope*—and the London and tour productions of *Best Little Whorehouse.*

Spisak went on to design costumes on his own for such films as *Q and A* and *January Man,* as well as the Broadway production of *Stepping Out* and the PBS series *Roanoak,* for which he received an Emmy nomination. He then moved into production design for such films as *Dying Young, Pacific Heights, Full Moon in Blue Water* and *Tigertown.*

In a phone interview from Calgary, where he was designing a show, Spisak spoke of the extraordinary team effort that made working on *Bountiful* one of his most memorable experiences.

175

What is the first thing you do when you're working on a film or play?

I start with the script. After I read *Trip to Bountiful* I went to Houston, where the story was set. It was important to go there because there is a sensibility about Texas.

How would you define that?

There's a pride about Texas and the land. The people have a sense of pride about their achievements and there is a strong connection between them. There's also this sense of city versus country, which is very important in the script.

There is a whole history of raising cattle, of farming, of building the cities. And there's a feeling that Texas is separate from the rest of the entire world. They are very special unto themselves.

But before knowing all that, I went to Houston and spent a couple of days looking at archives. I wanted to understand what 1947 Houston was about. It was already quite a good-sized city and a lot was happening, which was really fascinating. The library people were wonderful. I started to understand a little about the architecture, about the city's commerce, and about the migration to and from the city.

What did you learn about the architecture?

You usually think of the South or the West as being a certain way. But Houston was very much in tune with the rest of the country. There was also this ethereal quality against this sort of hard-edged quality, which I think came out in the script.

Once you finish your research what do you do next?

I search for some sort of inspiration for what I call a hook to hang things on. And Edward Hopper, besides being one of my favorite painters, really became that hook. You know his painting of the nude woman sitting on the bed? Although it isn't a direct translation to Geraldine's character, the feeling of that painting, that sort of loneliness, and that sort of urban saturation, spoke to me. A light went on, and I said, "This is the right idea. Now what's the opposite of this?" And then it became Andrew Wyeth. I went initially to Pete [Masterson] with these ideas.

"Every single thing that went into that space went in for a reason or with a purpose." Above, Carlin Glynn as Jessie Mae.

So you were the one who came up with the Hopper idea.

Oh, yeah, that was my thing. That was my mission—to find a way to communicate to everybody the feelings that I had about Texas and that time period after doing all this research. Pete, of course, fell in love with the Hopper idea, and we started looking at all of Hopper's paintings. Fred Murphy and I then began to develop the color scheme for the apartment, because that is the initial setting that we see—the city world which provides a contrast to what happens at the end of the movie: Geraldine's return to her farmhouse.

What was the color scheme that you developed?

A very saturated sort of jewel tone with harsh shadows and light for the city. Then we did watercolor and an ethereal kind of light for the country, which worked really well. Gary [Jones] knew exactly what he was doing with the palette, Fred knew what to do with the light, I knew what to do with the architecture and scenery, and Pete, of course, was thrilled because we had exactly the right feeling for the scenes in the city versus the scenes in the country. And then we could sort of feather everything in between. The last bus station scene was still pretty saturated in terms of color and that sort of spare Hopper kind of idea. That's one of my favorite pieces in the whole script.

Was it the set that you responded to so strongly?

No, I don't know if it was the set as much as it was the way the whole scene came together, with Geraldine against that wall, feeling desperate. It's a production designer's dream come true because it has all the right elements.

What are those elements?

It has to do with being able to give the director exactly what he's thinking in terms of the whole picture. It's seeing that the cameraman has the same idea and that you're able to feed one another. It's giving the cameraman the right light, the right space, the right conditions for him to do what he feels is right for the piece. And for that to happen the costume and production designers have to be in sync with each other, which can be difficult—because even though they're all working together, they're not always thinking the same thing. So things don't always connect the way they should.

Also, the budget comes into play.

Yes, and with *Bountiful* we were on a tight budget. And of course a favorite thing that producers like to say is, "Oh, it will stimulate your creativity, you'll have to come up with other

A Neil Spisak drawing for set design of *The Trip to Bountiful*.

ways of doing it." That's one take on it. Sometimes that does happen and sometimes it doesn't. We would not have been able to make the film for either the time or the money or the quality if everybody that was involved with the piece did not have that sort of Texas sensibility of doing something that's really wonderful and being proud of it.

Where are you from?
I'm originally from Ohio. But I live in Pennsylvania now.

How would you define the difference between Texas and other parts of the country?
I'm not sure I'm qualified to do that. It's a very hard thing to describe. And when you make the statement, there's always a million other things that contradict it. But what we're talking about is the people. Ann Roth, who was my mentor, taught me the importance of people. So I always start with the characters, the script and what the people are doing. I see so many projects which focus on the scenery and the visuals, but they forget about

the characters. You just see scenery for scenery's sake. One of the most helpful things to me was just spending time with Geraldine.

What about Horton Foote? Did you have a lot of contact with him?

No, but I did have one very big and bizarre moment with him that happened during the project. I remember it so clearly. It had to do with the apartment, which we built on a sound stage. I designed it in New York where I had a draftsman. Pete and I had lots of meetings. Then we built a model and Fred and I worked out what we wanted to change.

We talked about the surroundings, like what you see out the windows, which is a very big deal when you're doing a set, you know. And then, of course, the whole process of designing a set that goes on stage is different than a location because you're literally building from the ground up. You're doing it all. With a location set, you tend to adapt, fix and change what you already have. So, it's a different process.

Had you designed a set like that before?

Not much. It was one of the first big sets that I put on stage as a designer. And since it was such a naturalistic piece, if anything was wrong it really would have jumped out and would have been a big mistake. I was very concerned about it. And I was also nervous about Horton's reaction.

Did you know him very well?

No, I had not met him. Of course I'd been hearing about Horton for months because of Pete. So when the day came when the set was finally finished and we were supposed to meet, I was very nervous. I remember Horton walked in, looked around, sat down in the big armchair and about a minute and a half later he was asleep!

What was your reaction?

I was elated because I thought, "Well, he's at home, he's comfortable, and he gets it." So then I went on about my business. But that made me feel like I had hit it. Because it's hard to create a "real" feeling even though we live in it every day. What is real when you're starting with a void? It's sort of an interesting concept.

You start with nothing and then how long does it take for you to create a set that someone like Horton feels so at home in?

To actually construct it, it took about 3 1/2 weeks and a week to paint it. It actually took longer than everyone thought, by a day or two. But we were still on schedule.

Where did you build it?

We had a great shop in Texas and a great decorator. You see, at the same time that you're designing the set you're also thinking about what pieces and props you're going to need. The whole process doesn't really happen until you have a decorator and a lead man and their whole crew. Derek Hill was our decorator. I would describe basically what I wanted, and then he would give me different options. Sometimes I would look at his choices through Polaroids and sometimes I would go and look at them directly. The idea is to have as many things presented as you can, because at that point you're spinning in so many directions. Anyway, he found all of the stuff, and we would just pick and choose.

Which pieces or props were the most helpful to you creatively?

Every piece. Every single thing that went into that space went in for a reason or with a purpose. The twin beds were a major statement about the couple. John's dresser was selected because we felt it was something he carried with him from childhood, something he had forever. Carlin's dressing table was as up to date as it possibly could be, and she would have nudged and gotten something that she probably couldn't really afford.

To make her feel more glamorous.

Well, it's her extravagance—it's her idea of glamour. It's what she thinks is right, it's what she's seen in movie magazines.

What about the other pieces of furniture?

Well, there was also a very conscious effort on Pete's part that there not be much in terms of anything that really belongs to

Mother Watts. The idea was that she doesn't fit in this space.

Which would then isolate her a little bit more.
Yeah, exactly. I mean the idea of the three of them in that space is just sort of frightening. It's hard for me to imagine. I know it happened all the time, of course, and it still does. But it was amazing that they got along as well as they did considering they were on top of each other in that way.

The radio also seemed like an important part of that world.
Yes. The music was very important. And the fact that everything was put together in a strange kind of way contributed to the overall picture. Jessie Mae's dresser was sort of an odd piece that was stuck in the corner. And the apartment itself was a broken-up piece of a house, two rooms. The kitchen wasn't even a proper kitchen. It was stuck inside one of the rooms.

If you really tore the apartment apart, you would see that it probably was a living room and dining room. There's a door behind one of the beds that's obviously closed off, again to give the sense of confined space. And there's a hope chest in the bedroom, that was very specific in trying to say something.

You had doors with lace curtains.
Right. Well, that was more of a period detail. That happened a lot back then. You also often had double doors between the living room and dining room during that period. And for our purposes, that meant that you could technically see from room to room. And you could see the light and the shadows beyond. You never got the sense that either party had any privacy.

That claustrophobic sense was key to the whole story.
Absolutely.

Did the actors make any suggestions to you about the set or the design or the furniture?
Yes. Geraldine and I had several discussions. Basically, the uncomfortableness of her in the space was what she was interested in. So we wanted to *not* supply her with things. In terms of Carlin's character, there were very specific things that we did.

Such as?

There was a hobnail piece of glass on her vanity, something that she particularly wanted because she felt it was something she would have from her childhood. Carlin felt it inspired her as Jessie Mae. There was also a diaphragm in the drawer of the nightstand, between their beds. That was Carlin's idea, and it really gave that scene a whole other feeling.

You mean just knowing that the diaphragm was there?
Yeah, for her. No one else would ever know that.
We also did all period cosmetics. And her drawers were filled with the proper lingerie and sachets and that kind of stuff, which helped her deal with her character.
We filled everything. I mean there were empty drawers where they were supposed to be. We felt that Mother Watts just didn't have much and that was a choice we made. But even the empty drawers were lined with period newspaper.

And did that help the actors relate more to the time and the parts they were playing?
Yes. I also knew we would see the newspaper when Geraldine packs up to go. The point is to give the actors an environment that is safe, so they feel secure enough to try something new or whatever they feel like doing at that moment.

So you had to make the setting very real.
Absolutely. It had to be, because if you put the character of Jessie Mae as Carlin conceived her, and Pete and Horton conceived her, into some sort of artificial environment, she'd become a joke.

There is a strong sense of believability about this film. The audience really does care about each character.
Yeah, it's amazing how many people relate to this movie.

What props did you choose for John Heard's character?
You know this is embarrassing but . . .

You don't remember?
Right. I do remember a few objects like his wallet and his pocket knife and his watch. The pocket knife was on his dresser. It never was seen really, but it was one of those things that, as I

remember, we decided was something his father had given him, or it was his father's and his mom gave it to him.

What about Rebecca De Mornays's character—is there anything you want to say about her in terms of your work?

Well, Rebecca was probably the most unrelated to any of the spaces. In a sense, she just floated through the different spaces. And in contrast to that was the contained world of her suitcase. So from a design point of view, where her character came from had more to do with Gary than with me. That sense that she was really from somewhere else came more from her acting than any of the environments she was in. So there really wasn't much that I could do to help her.

Were there any times that you can remember when one person's vision clashed with another?

No. We were in sync. It was great.

You talked about your set in the city. What about the house you used in the country?

Actually, Horton found that house. And there were cattle literally standing in the living room when I went to look at it. It was completely derelict, completely falling apart, and we took our crew out there and rebuilt it.

How did you change it?

The structure and setting of the house were basically the same. But we planted grass all around it and let it grow. And we kept the cows out and rebuilt all the floors. And then we basically painted it with dye, like a watercolor wash. So the house was actually purple and green and blue and pink—it was all sort of very pastel transparent washes.

Did red ever come into play?

Well, Gary loves red. It's in all his work, and he uses it very well. Many directors are very afraid of red. You say red and they sort of get crazy. When you use red you have to have to do it very carefully because it becomes very important.

You mentioned using something like a watercolor wash. How did that tie in with your vision of Hopper?

In this case we tried to go with the opposite of the Hopper idea, into the Andrew Wyeth watercolor idea. Actually there were discussions about how far to go. Like what would Geraldine feel when she went back home and how desperate did you want the house to be when you were done? And the answers to that are really a matter of opinion. Frankly, the real house probably would have been far more dilapidated than the house in the film had it been deserted as long as it was supposed to have been. But on the other hand, we wanted it to feel like a wonderful place.

Did Pete Masterson say anything that inspired you?
Definitely. We had endless conversations about Geraldine not having things. Or we talked about Jessie Mae's inspiration coming from the movie magazines, or how Lootie withdrew but also tried to hold it together. Pete is a major Texan himself, and having worked with him before, I knew that the way he is, he would provide an inspiration for doing this project. He has a sort of calmness about things.

You said the first thing you do is to look at the script. What's the second step?
Meeting with the director. You read the script and then the two of you talk about what you think you may want. But it could end up that four weeks later it's completely different. The Edward Hopper thing didn't hit until a couple of weeks later. And then sometimes you actually go to the setting where the movie really takes place, like with *Bountiful*. Then you have to do the research, so you know what questions to ask.

Did you have a special feeling for the time period of the movie?
I was not around then, but it's very interesting to understand the kind of patriotism that existed during that period of time. It was sort of odd for me because the Vietnam War was certainly not that. But the late '40s were a very interesting time. It was about people trying to find their home again, and a "let's get it back together" period. There was a lot of construction, and things were changing.

And how did that tie in with Geraldine's plight?

In a sense it was the opposite. Geraldine wasn't trying to find her home. She was returning to all of those memories that she had. She had a life then, and for some reason or another she didn't click when she came into town. She didn't find her niche.

Just like the people in Hopper's world.
Exactly. There's a loneliness and a sort of urban saturation.

What do you need to be most creative—to truly create that sense of isolation that Geraldine felt, for instance?
The team, definitely. I need to be part of a team.

So, in a sense, to create Geraldine's isolation you need the opposite for yourself—to be part of something.
Right. I mean, if everybody's making the same movie, or if they're all making just a slightly different movie—which is just as good because you get all sorts of opinions—it's a wonderful thing. As far as I'm concerned, that's what it's all about.

Acknowledgements

The interview subjects themselves, of course, are the most praiseworthy individuals connected with this project. They were generous with their time and candid with their responses. We thank them all. Equal thanks go to those subjects who do not appear here. We hope to include many in future volumes.

DMB&B, the advertising company, was mother and father to *CREATIVITY: Conversations with 28 Who Excel* and *CREATIVITY IN FILM: Conversations with 14 Who Excel*. Without the agency's interest in the creative process and its abiding curiosity about creative people, these interviews would not have occurred.

Special appreciation goes to Al Hirschfeld, who provided readers not only with remarkable and delightful insights, but also with some of his unique drawings. The Margo Feiden Galleries, and David Leopold, went out of their way to provide the ones we needed.

Editorial assistant Abigail List made an invaluable contribution in checking facts, recontacting interviewees, deciphering muffled passages on audio tapes and giving the manuscript a critical read.

The number of individuals who were helpful is too large to allow full and proper acknowledgement. Several, however, must be mentioned.

Donna Lee was responsible for our finally being able to track down the reluctant Morgan Freeman, who so amazingly refuses to believe that his contributions to a drama are of a creative nature.

Carlin Glynn made it possible for us to reach the people who came together to make *The Trip to Bountiful*.

And a special thanks to Allan Bateman, a uniquely creative individual, for his endless hours of brainstorming, support and feedback.